MINIMALISM
A TO Z

Find joy, contentment, and purpose in life with minimalism

KAREN TREFZGER

creator of Maximum Gratitude, Minimal Stuff

Minimalism A to Z:
Find joy, contentment, and purpose in life with minimalism

ISBN-13: 978-1-6972-3203-5

**To Jon –
who makes it possible.**

Table of Contents

Introduction: Why Minimalism?

It seems we're all in the same boat. Busy – so busy. Stressed. Overwhelmed. Barely keeping up with the job, the house, the kids, and the chores.

However, we spend hours every day watching TV, and even more time online. And we do a lot of shopping.

We're especially prone to buying on impulse, some of us to the tune of thousands of dollars per year. Maybe it's a survival instinct ("I have to grab this now, even if I don't need it, because it might not be around later!"). Maybe it's the need to feel in control ("I want it, I can get it. It's *mine* now!").

Maybe we get addicted to the endorphins and dopamine our brains release when we buy something new. Unlike other types of addiction, this one is socially acceptable. We can't show up at a party and brag "I'm already drunk and high!" But we can say, "Look at these great shoes I just got on sale!" Even if we already have dozens of pairs, the new ones will be met with exclamations of approval.

So we also buy new stuff to bolster our self-esteem, numb our sad emotions, or pave the way to an imaginary brighter future.

Whatever the reason, with the advent of online shopping, we can now order items 24/7/365. With free two-day shipping, we can have something new delivered every day. It's so easy to acquire much more than we need or even want. We go way past the point of fulfillment and start to feel burdened.

Our world is full of messages that tell us more is always better and that we can buy our way to happiness. But our true needs are often ignored, buried under a pile of excess things and relentless busyness.

Minimalism means living with less clutter, busyness, debt, and stress so we have room for what really matters to us.

There are many reasons to explore minimalism, and the "why" will be slightly different for everyone. Figuring out your "why" is key to finding motivation and endurance when you encounter obstacles in your minimalist path. So settle in with a cup of tea or coffee and a notebook and pen, and think about what has motivated you to consider minimalism.

8 Reasons to Choose Minimalism

1. You're stressed and overwhelmed, and you're hoping minimalism will help you find order and peace.

You can't find your keys or your sunglasses or the permission slip you're supposed to sign. You can't clean the house without moving a bunch of clutter so you can vacuum, and you hate dusting all the knickknacks. You can't walk down the hall without tripping on one of your kid's toys. You can't shut your dresser drawers. You can't cook a meal without shoving things down the counter to make room to chop an onion. You can't sit at the table to eat anyway, because it's covered with a week's worth of mail, kids' homework, your purse, a water bottle, and (oh, there they are) your keys.

2. You're in debt and juggling the bills, and you're hoping minimalism will help you get your money under control.

You shop to reward yourself, to relax, or because you're bored. You don't need or use half the stuff you buy, and the debt keeps piling up. You feel burned-out by work, but still can't make ends meet.

3. You're overwhelmed with activities, and you're hoping minimalism will help you use your time more effectively.

Your schedule is jam-packed, and you feel guilty every time you say "no," so you just keep adding more commitments. You want to give your kids every opportunity, and you're afraid of missing out on something important, so you go-go-go every day. You're craving a real day off and some extra sleep.

4. You don't converse any more, you just discuss logistics, and you're hoping minimalism will help you deepen your relationships.

You really believe that people are more important than things, but if you're honest, you know you give more attention to your phone than you do to your loved ones. You spend more time thinking about what to buy or see or do next than you spend being fully present with anyone. Your "family time" consists of doing chores around the house, rushing to kids' lessons and games, and shopping.

5. You've developed some health issues, and you're hoping minimalism will help you focus on the needs of your body and your spirit.

Maybe it's too many late nights, maybe it's too much fast food, maybe it's too many desserts to reward yourself or too many drinks to numb yourself, but you realize something's got to change before your health is permanently compromised.

6. You've become focused on what you don't have, and crabby about all that is expected of you, and you're hoping minimalism will give you a new mindset.

Feeling deprived and dissatisfied is the pits. You want to learn gratitude and optimism before the frown lines are indelible.

7. You've become so used to buying whatever is "hot" that you're starting to feel like someone's puppet, and you're hoping minimalism will help you figure out what you really want.

You've been chasing goals that never fulfill you for long. You want to start thinking for yourself.

8. You want your life to amount to more than work and spend, work and spend, and you're hoping minimalism will help you make a difference.

You already know you can't buy your way to happiness. Spending less means it's possible to save and give more. You want that feeling of having money to spare, because you suspect that having room in your budget for generosity is the ultimate wealth.

Minimalism can help you create a life with more of what you love, and less of what you don't.

Are you ready to start living with more freedom and intention? This book will consider some basics that can help you get started today.

1. Attention

Don't let this happen to you: A day when you let texts and emails distract you. When you get lost down a rabbit hole of click bait and YouTube videos. When you binge on Netflix all evening. A day spent indoors except when walking to and from your car. When you eat quickly with no attention to what you are putting into your body. When you postpone dealing with a couple of important tasks, tasks you already put off yesterday and the day before. A day when you buy something on a whim, something that simply adds to your clutter.

A wasted, mindless day.

Mindlessness squanders your life with busyness and distraction. Find gratitude, purpose, and joy by increasing your attention.

12 Steps to Increasing Attention

1. Breathe deeply, stretch, and pray or meditate as soon as you awaken.

2. Eat healthfully, possibly outside or at least near a window. Relish the flavor of your food; watch and listen to the wind, birds, trees, water, even the cars going by. Notice when you have eaten enough, and realize that you feel peaceful and grateful.

3. Take time to connect with your roommate, spouse, or kids.

4. Work at your most important tasks first, one at a time, giving each your full attention. Realize that if something is worth your time, it's worth doing well. Feel less anxiety and stress because you know you're giving your best efforts to the tasks that matter.

5. Don't be distracted by your phone as you stand in the kitchen making your lunch or boiling the pot for tea. Look at the sunlight shining on the floor. Taste the crisp flavors of your salad. Listen to the higher pitch of the kettle as it gets close to boiling, and smell the bergamot in your Earl Grey. Feel the warmth as you lift your cup.

6. Don't try to squeeze in more tasks than you realistically have time for, and accept that there will be occasional delays and mix-ups. Allow a bit of breathing room in your schedule so you don't need to be pushy or fear being late for an appointment.

7. Be aware of the people around you at the grocery store or bank. Put your phone away and pay attention; smile and look people in the eye. Stand straight and loosen your neck, noticing that you're more comfortable when you don't slump. Is the person who serves you bored or stressed? Pleasantly acknowledge and thank him.

8. Observe your surroundings. Pay attention to what you see, hear, feel, smell, and taste. Look for beauty, no matter how small.

9. Be a good listener as you spend time with your family. Share your own successes and struggles, and receive congratulations and encouragement from your loved ones. Realize how much each one means to you.

10. Relax by doing something creative, by getting outside, or by moving your body. These activities are far more rewarding than an evening in front of the TV.

11. Prepare for bed by writing in a gratitude journal. Make a list of important tasks for tomorrow, releasing any worry or concern about them for the night. Breathe deeply, stretch, and pray or meditate.

12. Sleep well and peacefully so your body, mind, and spirit will be refreshed for tomorrow.

Congratulations! You should be feeling more calm, centered, and focused, with more energy for important relationships and tasks.

For best results, remember:

1. You don't have to buy an app or find a guru to learn mindfulness. You don't need to squeeze one more thing on your to-do list. Mindfulness takes no money and needs no appointment. You simply need to pay attention.

2. Don't worry if mindfulness feels strange at first. It's probably very different from the way you usually race through your days without thinking or noticing, but every time you practice, it will be easier to be aware.

3. Accept your emotions, good and bad, high and low. Notice when you start negative self-talk or when you have feelings like envy or impatience. We have to recognize and acknowledge these things if we want to replace them with something more positive.

4. Take time to be in nature. It's restorative.

5. Experience each season at it occurs, instead of following the retail calendar, which features bikinis in January and Halloween in August. This will not only ground you in the real world, it will reduce the feeling that time is rushing by or that each day is blurring into the next.

6. Use all of your senses to experience the world. Don't limit yourself to a screen.

7. Designate specific times to handle email and social media. You'll find this makes you more efficient and effective. Then you can get back to real life.

8. You will receive far more satisfaction from doing a kindness for one person than from clicking 100 "like" buttons.

9. Be thoughtful about which responsibilities you accept, and learn to say no. This will enable you to experience less stress while you devote your best energy and ideas to the tasks you care most about.

10. Don't shun silence. Periods of silence allow us to sort out other people's goals, interests, and priorities from our own. When we turn our attention away from ads, news, and social media, we can start to make decisions that meet our deepest needs.

Now you're really on your way to a joyful life!

2. Buy Less

Want to reduce clutter permanently? Stop buying so much.

We all know that, right? So why is it so hard to do?

Maybe it's difficult because it sounds like taking a step backward in life. In a culture where success is often measured in terms of material possessions, buying less sounds boring, old-fashioned, and a little ridiculous.

And since we're all exposed to hundreds of ads every day, in every possible space and format, we're constantly aware of the world of products available for our consumption. Even if we tune out most of the details, our cultural atmosphere is permeated with the message "buy, buy, buy!"

I own a lot less than I used to. I have more time and money available to me than ever before. Because I own fewer things, I spend less energy cleaning, managing, and organizing. I spend less time shopping. I have more opportunity to pursue my greatest passions, however I decide to define them.

But there are some areas where I still struggle with spending too much. I can't pass up a book store, and my husband and I eat way too often in restaurants.

My weaknesses may be different from yours, but maybe there are some strategies that can help all of us.

8 Ways to Stop Buying So Much

1. Track your spending.

Many people make this suggestion, and I've tried it several times, only to become bogged down and give it up after a few weeks. What finally made it a useful strategy was to track spending in one problem area (for us it was eating out). Seeing in black and white how often we ate out and how much we spent gave us a ton of motivation to practice some self-control.

2. Don't look for ways to save money on items you don't really need to buy in the first place.

When I get a coupon for 25% off any item at my favorite book store, I suddenly feel a compulsion to buy, even if I don't have a particular book in mind. Buy-one-get-one posters try to lure me in. Instead of looking for deals, rewards, or other ways to "save," just don't shop until you need to. Stick with the couch you already have, the clothes you already own, and the car you just paid off.

3. Eliminate shopping triggers.

Unsubscribe from store emails. Unlike brands on Facebook. Change your route home if you drive by a store or restaurant you tend to visit. You get the idea. Out of sight, out of mind. By not having the visual reminder, you can change your routine and break your habit.

4. Start with a fixed amount of cash each week.

Pay bills online or with a check. The cash is for groceries and other food, gas, and incidentals. Challenge yourself to make it last.

5. Don't carry a credit card.

This is a corollary to #4. Keep your credit card at home where it can't be whipped out on impulse (I seal mine in an envelope and file it with my credit card statements). You can always retrieve it for a true emergency.

6. Plan ahead.

My husband and I eat out less if I have dinner planned and ingredients ready to go. You might curb spending on clothes if you take time before each new season to look at what you already own, and plan to purchase only what you need to fill in gaps.

7. Use the "seven day rule."

Impulse buying will not only blow your budget, it will fill your house with clutter. Notice what you see and want to buy, and tell yourself that if you still want it in seven days you can come back and buy it guilt-free. Do you even remember it a week later? Or does your sudden "need" dissipate during that time?

8. Redirect the time you spend shopping.

Minimalism isn't just about having less or buying less. It's also about having more time to do things that add value to your life. So instead of spending time shopping, take the time to learn something new, to connect with a friend, to get more exercise, or to pursue a hobby. Spend time riding your motorcycle rather than buying accessories for it. Spend time creating art rather than shopping for the latest décor.

> To have what we want is riches,
> but to be able to do without is power.
>
> George MacDonald

3. Clear the Clutter

Imagine your dream home.

Open the front door, step inside, and look around. What do you see?

You probably *don't* see stacks of movies on the coffee table or toys scattered over the floor. You don't see a kitchen counter too crowded for meal prep, or a dining table so cluttered that no one can eat there. You don't see piles of mail, laundry, dirty dishes, unfinished repairs, or things that need to be cleared away before you can sit down.

You see the beautiful home you'd love to have.

Unfortunately, it can be hard to get started with the difficult job of reducing the amount of stuff we've accumulated over the years. As much as we might want to live with only the things that "spark joy," that also means we have to deal with all of the things that *don't*, things we don't really want or need, things that weigh us down and make us feel stressed or unhappy.

But that relaxing home is not an impossible dream. And there isn't just one "right way" to clear the clutter. Try one or more of these strategies.

18 Ways to Clear the Clutter

1. Start with the most visible.

Tackle stuff on counter tops or the floor, for example. Leave closets and drawers for later. You'll see immediate positive results, which will increase your energy and confidence. Visible progress will help sustain your decluttering efforts.

2. Do one thing to make life easier.

- Are you always searching for your keys? Put a hook for them near the door, or clear clutter from your purse and designate one pocket for keys.

- Is the TV remote always buried? Declutter some throw pillows from the couch, clear out a drawer to give it a permanent home, or clear off the coffee table and place a tray or basket for it there.

- Do coats, backpacks, and shoes always end up on the kitchen table or strewn across the floor? Declutter the front closet so there's plenty of room to hang coats, and put up some heavy-duty hooks for backpacks. Place a basket on the floor of the closet for outdoor shoes.

- Are your sink and counter always full of dirty dishes? Take three minutes each morning to empty the dishwasher, and help everyone practice the habit of putting dirty dishes into it. No room to put clean dishes away? Sort and declutter the 27 plates, 23 bowls, 18 mugs, 9 cooking pots, and piles of utensils that overfill your kitchen cupboards and drawers. (Hint: the plates, bowls, mugs, utensils, and pots and pans you had to wash are probably your favorites.)

3. Start with big items.

Do you need a couch *and* a love seat *and* three chairs? Can you mount the TV on the wall and remove the entertainment center? What about that table covered in junk mail? If all it does is collect clutter, remove it, and dump the junk in the recycling bin. Do you need four bookcases? Declutter unloved books and trinkets, and maybe you can remove one or more. Do you need a hutch *and* a sideboard? Declutter unused china, linens, and miscellany at the back of the cupboard, and maybe you can delete one piece of furniture. You might love the space far more than you love the stuff.

4. Start small.

Choose a drawer, a shelf, or a cupboard. Empty it completely. Sort stuff into three categories: keep, donate, or toss. Clean the area, and return only the items you use and love. Organizing is easier now that you've removed the excess.

5. Do it all at once.

Take the next several weekends, or a week's vacation, and declutter all at once. Work room by room or category by category. Stay hydrated. Take a short break every couple of hours to eat, stretch, or simply close your eyes. Stop each evening and do something fun and relaxing, such as going out for dinner or a movie, taking a bike ride, or having a soak in the tub and an early bedtime.

6. Do it little by little.

Slow and steady isn't glamorous, but it might be more thoughtful and sustainable. Start with the easy stuff, like duplicates and items in storage that you've basically forgotten you own. Each thing you part with will give you the strength and motivation to let go of the next, and like a snowball, the effect will grow.

7. Take a picture.

To you, a room might seem "cozy" rather than cluttered, but a photo will help you see the space with fresh eyes. Looking at a picture changes your perspective and allows you to be more detached. It could be the perfect tool to clarify what needs to be cleared away. Be sure to take an "after" photo as well, so you can see and celebrate what you've accomplished.

8. Pretend.

What if you were moving? Ask "Would I bother to wrap this item in bubble wrap, pack it, load it, haul it, carry it, unpack it, and find a place for it?" If the answer is no, declutter it.

9. Get real.

If you're paying for off-site storage, why? Unless you're taking a job overseas for a specified period of time, and plan to return afterwards to use all of your stuff, why are you renting storage space? My guess is that it's stuff you don't use, that won't fit in your home, that you inherited and don't want or need, or that belonged to your kids when they were small (and they don't want it or have room for it either). If you never need or want this stuff, or don't even remember what it is, why are you paying to store it? Contact a local auctioneer, and let it go.

10. Do a gut check.

Ask yourself, "If I didn't already own this thing, would I spend money to buy it today?" If not, let it go.

11. Ditch the guilt.

Do unfinished projects clutter your space? The quilt you barely started, the dresser you've been meaning to paint and restyle, the old bicycle you planned to refurbish? Here's the question: Do you want to work on this project *right now*? Will you schedule time within the next month to work on it? If not, abandon it and donate the stuff without guilt. Now you're free to consider a new project that actually excites you.

12. Look for hot spots.

Hot spots are places where clutter doesn't belong but tends to gather. Counters and tables are some of the obvious possibilities. Notice piles of mail, magazines, purses, backpacks, keys, and dirty dishes. Maybe there are baskets of laundry, whether dirty or clean, in the hallway. Does your car harbor trash, fast food cartons, and empty water bottles? Do cases of toilet paper or soft drinks never make it past the entry hall? Does the living room floor host discarded toys, scattered shoes, and pillows that are supposed to decorate the couch but actually crowd it? Start your work in one of these areas.

13. Choose a theme.

Declutter one category of items, such as clothes, books, toys, office supplies, kitchen equipment, makeup and toiletries, hobby supplies.

14. Do it by halves.

Is there a collection you fear parting with completely? What if you let go of half? This strategy can be very helpful for some of those hard-to-remove items such as books, souvenirs, family memorabilia and other collectibles.

15. Establish a quarantine.

Box up items you fear you'll need someday, and hide them away for a set period of time (say three to six months). If you haven't opened the box before the deadline, simply let it go. If there *is* anything you actually need, you'll realize it before you've given it away.

16. Overcome inertia.

Does that box of souvenirs really have sentimental value, or do you keep it out of laziness? Gretchen Rubin, author of *Outer Order, Inner Calm*, writes about an interesting paradox: having fewer mementos may actually help us enjoy more memories. Rather than being overwhelmed by a stack of stuff we never actually look at, a carefully chosen keepsake stands alone and uncrowded, able to get the attention it deserves. So overcome your lethargy. Choose to display one great photo of a special night with your best college pals, and recycle the boxes of college notebooks and memorabilia.

17. Make a home.

Any item that is useful and valuable needs its own home. There should be no question about where the item belongs or where it can be found when it's not in use. It should always be easy to put your hands on useful items such as:

- your passport
- a flashlight
- a pair of scissors
- your checkbook
- a roll of toilet paper
- an extension cord
- the tweezers

- a postage stamp
- measuring spoons
- last year's tax return
- a working pen
- a clean kitchen towel

18. Prepare for the future.

Many years have passed, and your relatives have gathered to clear out your house after your death. Emotions aside, how difficult is it to complete this job? What items will they keep, sell, donate, recycle, or toss? Declutter now so you don't leave a headache for your children or grandchildren.

Think you have no time to declutter?
Do you have 10 minutes?
10 minutes a day times 7 days a week
times 52 weeks equals 3,640 minutes.
That's more than 60 hours.
You can do a lot in 60 hours!

4. Do Less

A lot of people think of "minimalism" as a huge white room with a white couch, a glass table, and some modern art.

And while that is one minimalist design aesthetic, and minimalists *do* talk a lot about decluttering, it would be a mistake to think that purging physical items (along with all color and personality) from your home is the ultimate goal.

Decluttering is a valuable tool that brings many benefits, but minimalism is a complete lifestyle that impacts much more than your physical space.

Blogger Emma Scheib of SimpleSlowLovely.com originally thought that minimalism was all about clearing the clutter. She eventually realized it's about much more – removing busyness and stress in order to focus on the things you personally value.

She writes:

> I [used to be] quick to answer "yes" to any new request for my time, resulting in an overflowing calendar. These "yes commitments" meant I was living under constant duress. I began to feel fearful of the life I was creating for myself. Thankfully, the concepts of minimalism taught me the importance of saying "no" and the courage to enforce personal boundaries that I'd never had before.

The conventional wisdom is that we must multi-task, we must be on the go, we must *push* to have a valuable life. We become too busy to be flexible, too busy to stop, to engage with others, to listen, to observe, to pay attention, to reflect, to imagine, or to properly rest.

Time and energy are finite, and you simply can't do it all. In truth, when you try to say "yes" to everything, when you let the Fear of Missing Out drive your schedule, you will experience burnout. And the blur of activity is not just stressful and tiring – it will make you feel that your life is racing past while everything important falls through the cracks.

Minimalism lets you focus.

It lets you breathe. It's about being intentional.

Advertisers work hard to convince you that you'll be more confident, happy, and fulfilled with the newest this or that. You work longer, shop more, and rest less in order to satisfy the cravings they create. But aren't you sick and tired of wasting your precious life on paying for, cleaning, organizing, and maintaining stuff?

When we choose to own less, we gain time. When we sign ourselves up for fewer activities, we have more time to create, learn, appreciate nature, and connect with family and friends. We must learn to say "no," even when it feels uncomfortable, and guard some open spaces on our calendars. We need to make time to do the things we love.

So consider social obligations, volunteer commitments, your children's extracurricular activities, and how you use your smart phone. Evaluate time spent on your beauty routine and in front of the TV.

Determine your favorite hobby and practice it exclusively for a month, taking a break from all the others. Does it bring you more satisfaction and enjoyment when you devote more time and energy to it? What if your children did the same with their favorite activity?

Choose the one volunteer effort that means the most to you. How much more could you further this cause by focusing on it?

Pick one or two social media platforms in which to participate, and ignore the rest for a month. Does this make you feel less stressed and distracted? If so, deactivate or delete the excess. Pare down your social engagements as well, and see if you enjoy connecting with others more when you feel less pressure and obligation.

How you spend your time defines who you are and who you become.

And for more quality time, savor the people, activities, and things that truly add meaning to your life, and minimize everything else.

My goal is no longer to get more done,
but rather to have less to do.

Francine Jay

35

Minimalist Inspiration: *The Story of the Mexican Fisherman*

Courtney Carver shared a version of this story in her book *Soulful Simplicity*.

∅

An American businessman was on vacation in a coastal Mexican village. He was lounging on the pier when a small boat piloted by one fisherman docked beside him. Inside the boat were several large yellowfin tuna. The businessman complimented the fisherman on their quality and asked how long it took to catch them.

The fisherman replied, "A couple of hours." This surprised the American. "Why not stay out longer and catch more?" he asked. "I have enough for the needs of my family," replied the Mexican. "Then what do you do the rest of the day?" wondered the businessman.

"I sleep late, fish a little, play with my children, and take siestas with my wife," replied the fisherman. "Later I stroll into the village, have a glass of wine in the cantina, and play guitar with my amigos. It's a full life."

The American scoffed at this. "I'm a Harvard MBA and I can help you," he said. "You should spend more time fishing, make more money, and buy a bigger boat. Then you can bring in even more fish, and eventually buy a fleet of boats. Put all your amigos to work! Cut out the middleman, deal directly with the processor, and use your profits to open a cannery. You'd have a monopoly on the product, the processing, and the distribution. You'd need to leave here and move to Mexico City, and as your corporation expands you might wind up in LA or New York City."

"How long would all of this take?" the fisherman wondered.

"Probably 15 or 20 years," replied the American. "When the time is right, you'd announce an IPO and sell your company stock to the public for millions of dollars. You'd have it made!"

"And then what?" asked the Mexican.

"You could move to a beautiful coastal village," the American enthused. "Sleep late, do a little fishing, play with your grandkids, take siestas with your wife, and stroll to the village in the evenings, where you could enjoy some wine and play guitar with your amigos."

5. Embrace Empty Space

Do you think you can't be a minimalist because you don't want to live with only enough possessions to fill a backpack?

You're in good company. The majority of aspiring minimalists don't choose that lifestyle. I live with my husband in a small apartment, but we have a couch and a coffee table and bookshelves and a queen-size bed and a dresser and a dining table with several chairs. My kitchen has a dishwasher and a microwave. I have art on my walls, houseplants, hobby supplies, and a TV.

But I also have something that I didn't have when my home was more cluttered, and that's empty space.

Before I decluttered, I didn't realize how much I would love empty space, because I'd always filled every space I had. Every shelf, every drawer, every cupboard, closet, wall, or shed was filled with stuff I was sure I needed (or would need someday) and valued (even if I didn't use it or look at it).

Once I had more space, I realized that space made me happy. I like a kitchen cupboard with only one set of dishes in it, or a bookshelf that doesn't have books stacked behind and on top of other books. I like not bumping into or tripping on things, or searching for them in piles of clutter. I can see, enjoy, and easily access the items I own.

I love it that my home looks and feels bigger.

Dana K. White, author of *Decluttering at the Speed of Life*, says that the secret to creating empty space is to start thinking of your home, and each room, closet, cupboard, and drawer in it, as a container.

The purpose of a container is to restrain, to limit, to prevent the spread of something. We can buy all kinds of containers: bins, boxes, baskets, and more. Then we fill all of those storage containers, and stack them up in our closets and cupboards. This hoard of organized stuff creates the illusion that there is no clutter, but sooner or later all the containers are full. Then we buy more containers to fill and organize, and squeeze them in. Does that sound familiar? It's what I did for years.

When we moved into a bigger house, we just filled it with more stuff. I was constantly looking for the perfect storage solution.

I eventually realized that I had way more stuff than I needed or wanted. Once I understood that my home was *itself* a container, and that the secret was not to pack it as full as possible, but to use it to help me set limits on my possessions, I found that I had plenty of space.

Take my clothes closet, for example. I wanted to be able to store my clothes without having them all squashed together, wrinkled, or falling off the hangers. I thought for a long time that my closet was just too small, and that I needed special multi-garment hangers or another clothing rod (additional "containers").

But when I emptied my closet, and put all of the pants together, and all of the dresses, and all of the skirts, jackets, tops, and shoes, I found that more than half of those pieces were things I never wore, and that probably no one needs six pairs of black sandals, and that button-down shirts always gap and pull, and that fitted jackets aren't my best look. When I removed the excess, and replaced the items I actually liked wearing, I had plenty of space. I could see at a glance what was available. I loved the empty floor and the space between each hanger.

Now, instead of filling each space in my home with as much as I possibly can, even if it looks organized, I choose the best, the most useful, my favorites. Those go in first, and when the space is full, **I know that everything else is less valuable to me than what's already there.**

And by "filling" the space, I don't mean stacking things high and cramming things in so that every cupboard or drawer is always ready to tumble out and bury me in an avalanche of junk.

The key to successful decluttering is to purge enough stuff that you only have what fits comfortably in the container of your home. You don't have to question whether something has worth, but whether it fits your container. Favorite things get first dibs on the space; things that don't have a current purpose don't. It's not an emotional decision, it's a practical one.

You don't need a bigger house. You need less stuff.

- If you love a painting, don't hang twelve other things on the wall. Leave empty space around it to show it off.

- If your kitchen counter is for preparing meals, don't crowd it with appliances, canisters, dishes, mail, or anything that will steal the space you need to chop veggies or bake cookies.

- If your couch is for relaxing, don't cover it with laundry, cat toys, and eight throw pillows. Leave empty space for more than one person to sit or recline.

Similarly, you don't need more hours in your day, you need to edit your activities and commitments.

- If you enjoy a hobby, make time to pursue it.

- If you value a relationship, leave space on the calendar for date night, and time during the day or evening to talk, listen, and cuddle.

- Don't let TV, social media, online shopping, or other distractions steal your time. Create limits ("containers") to preserve space for activities you believe are more important.

Embrace empty space, in your home and on your calendar. Release the things that don't add value to your life, and make space for what you cherish. Don't rush to fill empty spaces, but appreciate the clarity and peace they bring.

Simplicity boils down to two steps:
Identify the essential.
Eliminate the rest.

Leo Babauta

6. Financial Freedom

Here it is – the most important financial advice you'll ever receive:

Spend less than you earn.

If you cut back on spending, you'll be able to pay off debt, build an emergency fund, give more generously, and start saving for college or retirement or a trip to Europe. Spending less will reduce your stress levels and improve your sleep. It might even improve your marriage.

Spend less enables us to achieve financial freedom. But in a country where most of us live paycheck to paycheck and the average American has almost $7,000 of credit card debt, the message to *spend less* is clearly not getting through!

Minimalism is not about giving up all comforts and conveniences. But a minimalist does embrace the concept of *intentional* spending. Once you find balance by shedding the things you don't need so you can focus on the things that really matter to you, you realize that thoughtless or impulsive purchases burden and distract you. More than that, they steal your life energy.

"Your money or your life."

If someone thrust a gun into your ribs and said that sentence, what would you do? Most of us would turn over our wallets. The threat works because we value our lives more than our money.

Or do we?

As consumers, we act as if money has the capacity to meet all of our needs, wants, and desires. Most of us believe that if we had more money, we'd be happier and worry-free. That might be true if you live in poverty, but people with six-figure incomes feel the same way. We put a lot of faith in our money.

We need to remember that **money represents our life energy**.

When we go to our jobs, we trade our life energy for money. Life energy is our allotment of time here on earth. It's precious because it's finite and irretrievable, and because our choices about how we use it define the meaning and purpose of our lives.

So when we spend carelessly, or worse, use credit and spend money we don't yet have (thereby promising our *future life energy* in payment), we may be harming ourselves more than we realize. If we aren't receiving fulfillment, satisfaction, and value in proportion to the life energy we gave in exchange, we are the losers.

Financial freedom comes when you identify your true needs and consciously choose to purchase the items and experiences which fulfill those needs. If you squander your life energy on stuff that doesn't ultimately satisfy and support your values, you end up with a lot of clutter and a lot less life.

This isn't about guilt or deprivation. It's about honoring and valuing your life energy, a limited resource.

When you become conscious of unrewarding spending patterns, you can start to use money in ways that bring you more contentment and well-being. You'll realize that you have enough for survival, for comfort, and even for little luxuries. Everything you need, and nothing to weigh you down. You can appreciate and enjoy what money provides without purchasing anything that isn't needed or wanted. As the ancient Chinese book of wisdom, the *Tao Te Ching*, puts it:

"He who knows he has enough is rich."

This mindset also helps us avoid lifestyle inflation. Lifestyle inflation is the tendency we all have to increase our spending when income goes up. When we do this, it remains impossible to get out of debt, save, invest, contemplate changing careers, or work less. It forces us to keep working just so we can pay the bills. We may justify spending by saying "I work hard so I deserve this." But we're putting ourselves in financial bondage. What we really deserve is less debt, less stress, less clutter, more time, and more long-lasting satisfaction.

When we stop trying to buy happiness, we can start to discover our true calling and identity, which our culture usually equates with a job, but is so much more than that. When we gain financial freedom, we can use our life energy to build real wealth: knowledge, skills, creativity, relationships, community, gratitude, and generosity.

The cost of anything
is the amount of life you exchange for it.

Henry David Thoreau

Money may be the husk of many things
but not the kernel.
It brings you food, but not appetite;
medicine, but not health;
acquaintance, but not friends;
servants, but not loyalty;
days of enjoyment, but not peace or happiness.

Henrik Ibsen

7. Gifts That Matter

I used to use gift-giving as an excuse to shop.

I would feel the urge to buy something – anything really – just because it's "fun" to buy. (Oh yes, I understand a shopping addiction, and that little rush of pleasure when you acquire something new.)

So, to assuage my guilt (because I knew I didn't really need anything), I'd buy something as a gift. Maybe because one of my nieces or nephews really did have a birthday coming up, or because Mother's Day was just around the corner, or because I thought I'd save an item for Christmas. (I often had a closet full of gifts by October that I didn't remember purchasing and that I no longer felt excited about giving.)

A lot of debt is generated by gift-buying. Back in the day, I always had a few thousand dollars in credit card debt, largely due to spur-of-the-moment buying. I always justified it because much of it was stuff I bought for others, but I was usually spending money I didn't have.

Our culture tells us we should have what we want even if we can't afford it. We just buy now and pay later. We have "good" credit if we make our payments on time, even if we're carrying a staggering amount of debt. And the items end up costing a lot more when you factor in the interest.

What are we buying, anyway? Largely it's stuff that no one needs or wants. And since we all feel a certain amount of guilt when we get rid of gifts, they add to the clutter in our homes, increasing our feelings of stress and overwhelm.

We are spending money we don't have to buy things people don't want, which winds up filling our homes with clutter.

So let's try an experiment.

Ask your friends or family members about their favorite memories of birthdays or holidays. When I did this, people mentioned:

- solving clues in a "treasure hunt" for gifts

- annual trips to a mountain Christmas tree farm, roaming through the crisp winter forest to choose a tree, and sitting by the campfire with mugs of hot apple cider

- the holiday we stayed in the coastal town of Mendocino, and the ice cream shop on Main Street that opened up on Christmas morning to give free ice cream cones to passersby

- a birthday trip to San Francisco when we walked across the Golden Gate Bridge and visited the Exploratorium

- a birthday party held at a local tea shop, when all the girls wore fancy Victorian hats and feasted on tea, scones, and tiny sandwiches served on pretty china

- a late-October birthday party when every guest carved, decorated, and took home their own jack-o-lantern

No one mentioned actual gifts. Not one present was even remembered.

Think about your own favorite memories. Do they involve things you received, or things you experienced with friends and loved ones?

The most valuable gifts we can give are time and attention.

I don't care if your "love language" is giving gifts. That doesn't mean you need to buy a knickknack or a piece of jewelry to show your love.

The best gifts demonstrate how well you know someone and how much attention you pay to their interests. They also cost more than money – they take creativity, sensitivity, and effort. A heartfelt thank you letter might be a wonderful gift.

- Don't just give concert tickets to your parents; take them to the concert and enjoy talking about it afterwards.

- Don't just give your kid a pile of new toys; buy one toy you know he'll love, and then play with him.

- Don't just give a restaurant gift card to your friend; take her to lunch, or invite her into your home for a meal, and spend time reconnecting.

Bake cookies, plant a rose bush, or refurbish that used bicycle **together**. Go to a movie, break in new hiking boots, or get a massage **together**. Go somewhere you've never been, but always wanted to go, **together**. Turn your phone off, and focus on your shared activity.

When you give gifts that matter, you do more than avoid clutter and debt. You do more than throw a Pinterest-worthy party or attempt to wow with quantity or expense. You actually strengthen the relationship between yourself and your recipient, and create memories that last forever.

Everything can be taken away from a man
except what is hidden in his heart and mind.

Victor Frankl

8. Habits That Keep Life Simple

We're real people. We work, we socialize, we have hobbies and husbands and kids. Stuff enters our homes every day, and if we don't change the way we deal with it, clutter will reappear. So part of the minimalist lifestyle includes learning new habits that keep stuff from once again overwhelming our lives.

Here are four habits that will prevent the reappearance of clutter. Use them as minimalist mantras!

4 Minimalist Habits

1. Don't just put it down – put it away.

You've probably heard the old adage "A place for everything and everything in its place." As you declutter, make a home for each item you need, use, and love.

Items often end up "homeless" because we simply have too much stuff. If your bathroom counter is covered with bottles and potions, for example, you may just have too many. Get rid of the duplicates, and the things you used once and didn't like, and the outdated creams and remedies. Use the medicine cabinet and vanity drawers to store the things you need and use regularly, and try to keep the counter clear of everything except hand soap. It's not only more soothing and spa-like, it's far more sanitary.

Remember that organizing, by itself, isn't the same as decluttering. Simply organizing stuff in boxes and bins can hide the fact that we have too much clutter. Containers are meant to restrain and corral the items they hold. Containers such as drawers, cupboards, closets, spice racks, book cases, and shoe bags place limits on what we store. The answer is not to run out and buy more containers, it's to put your favorite items in the containers you have and declutter the lesser-loved items that don't fit.

Don't waste another minute searching for your misplaced phone or checkbook, or shuffling through drawers looking for your most comfortable and supportive bra. Find a home for these things, and never put them down except where they belong.

2. One in, one out.

When you purchase something new, discard something comparable. That way, your containers don't overflow and everything still has a home. For example, if you replace a worn pair of sandals, discard the old ones. New laptop? Recycle the old one. Don't waste all the time and effort you spent decluttering. Drop your habit of hanging on to old stuff you don't need.

3. Curb the impulse.

Shopping for the sake of entertainment, novelty, or on a whim is another habit that needs to stop. Nothing derails your decluttering efforts (and your budget) more quickly than impulse buys.

Be aware of your weaknesses. Are there certain stores you "can't resist?" Certain items you tend to collect? Has stopping at yard sales become a favorite form of entertainment? Awareness is an important part of changing habits. Several strategies may help: carry only cash, change your route so you don't drive by the alluring store, wait three (or seven, or thirty) days to see if you still want to purchase a tempting item.

Commit to buying less.

4. It's a lot easier to keep up than to catch up.

Develop routines for doing household chores, since piles grow when chores are neglected. It really takes just a couple of minutes to sort through the mail every day. The longer you wait, the bigger the pile gets and the more you dread the job. The same goes for doing dishes or folding laundry.

Do you put off a chore because you hate doing it? Try timing it. It may not take as long as you think, and once you realize that, it will be easier to make yourself do it. So many jobs take only five minutes (some take only one)! Or trade a chore you dislike with another household member's least favorite chore. My husband vacuums for me, and I never ask him to dust or pay the bills.

Your children benefit from learning to do chores, so teach them to help you. Make a list of jobs the kids can do weekly, such as sweep the front porch, strip beds and put dirty sheets in the laundry hamper, clean the bathroom mirror/counter/sink, or tidy and dust living room tables. Have them rotate responsibilities each week.

Create daily habits for yourself and your kids. Be specific about what you want them to do, such as "Make your bed (at least pull up bedclothes neatly and put the pillow at the head)," "Put clean clothes away and dirty ones in the hamper," "Hang up your towel," and "Put toys where they belong." These habits should become just as routine as "Brush your teeth" and "Wash your hands."

Instead of letting the house get really dirty and cluttered, and then having to spend a lot of time and effort cleaning it up, make it a habit to clean as you go. You'll reduce mess, stress, and arguments, and keep your newly decluttered home spacious and serene.

Gretchen Rubin, author of *The Happiness Project*, reminds us that "What you do every day matters more than what you do once in a while." It's the daily events, habits, routines, and attitudes that determine the direction of our lives.

Decluttering can be a Herculean task. When minimalist habits become your daily lifestyle, you'll never have to do a huge declutter again!

A small daily task – if it be really daily –
is worth more than the labor of
a spasmodic Hercules.

Anthony Trollope

Minimalist Inspiration:
Stoicism

The Stoics believed that our happiness depends on our mindset, and that negative feelings like worry, fear, anger, and jealousy could be managed and minimized. While recognizing that life is full of difficulties and uncertainty, they taught that the best way to remain at peace is to let go of things we can't control (such as other people and external events) and focus on the things we can (our own thoughts and reactions).

This ancient school of thought is a practical philosophy for living a good life. By encouraging us to remain humble, ethical, and satisfied with the blessings we already have, Stoicism complements modern minimalism.

No one can be poor that has enough,
nor rich, that covets more than he has.

Seneca (4 BC - AD 65)

∅

No man is free who is not master of himself.

Epictetus (AD 55-135)

9. Identity – It's Not What You Own

We all need love, acceptance, community, and a sense of accomplishment. These factors contribute to our mental health and self-esteem.

Psychologists such as Abraham Maslow have demonstrated that once our basic physical needs are met, we embark on a path to self-improvement. Whether that leads us to seek out new experiences, new skills, new possessions, or a new look, we always want something more and different.

This drive has a positive side. Invention and innovation have always come from the urge to be and do more and better. Dissatisfaction with the status quo has created tools, machines, art, music, democracy, and movements for human rights and social justice.

But it doesn't always lead to happiness.

Unfortunately, the desire to "be all you can be" also fuels discontent. I know you've felt it, when everything you've already done or acquired feels like old news.

We're always trying to enhance our looks, our wardrobes, our jobs, our homes, or our relationships, but once the initial happiness of acquisition wears off, we start looking for the next new thing. That dopamine high is short-lived! We compare and compete with others, and keep searching for things or experiences to compensate for our perceived inadequacies. We may try to gain significance through

- designer clothes
- the latest phone or smart gadget
- liposuction and Botox
- a luxury car
- a remodeled kitchen
- a diploma from an elite college
- a promotion and a prestigious title
- exotic travel

We may get everything we thought we wanted, everything we genuinely desired at some point. But those items eventually fade into background noise, things we don't really notice or appreciate any more, part of what we have to clean, store, insure, repair, upgrade, work at, or continue to pay for. Then we need something new to bring back the excitement.

If we equate our belongings and experiences with our value as persons, we enter a never-ending quest for acceptance and respect. We must continually prove our worth. We try to satisfy our very real emotional and psychological needs with the temporary high of new stuff.

Advertisers prey on these needs, of course. But the real problem may be that it's much easier to *buy* something than it is to accomplish something. It's much easier to *look* successful than to expend the time, energy, attention, and commitment it takes to leave the world a better place.

Our culture confuses material possessions with real achievement. But that constant pursuit can leave us feeling hollow and unsatisfied.

4 Ways to Break Free of the Drive to Acquire

1. Identify your true need.

Your pursuit of the next purchase, experience, or program for self-improvement is about an internal need. What is that need, really? Are you buying a new car to prove you are worthy of respect? Do you need a designer handbag to feel a part of the group? Figure out your intangible emotional need.

2. Determine a way to actually meet that need.

If a pair of shoes is giving you self-esteem, that's a problem. What is a true solution to your need? If you lack self-worth, maybe you need therapy, or a life coach, or an activity that bolsters your confidence and makes you feel needed. Buying something won't do that.

3. Separate your identity from your stuff.

If we believe our possessions or experiences indicate our value, we become slaves to those things. And if times change, whether by job loss, age, or some other factor, and we have to give up those things, a piece of our self-worth and identity will go with them.

4. Focus on what really matters.

The desire to thrive is a noble one, and it shouldn't be wasted in seeking a fancier house or a bigger wardrobe. Remain ambitious, but choose goals that are worthy of you. Strive to create, to contribute, to be healthy, wise, courageous, playful, and compassionate.

We don't have to be caught in an eternal loop of desire and discontent, mere consumers who are constantly enticed into buying something new. We don't have to be so busy trying to impress everyone else that we ignore our true needs. Minimalism can help us find lasting satisfaction.

We can reduce the clutter in our homes and schedules, gaining peace and confidence. By keeping only what we value, we actually gain a clearer understanding of ourselves, and simplify our lives at the same time.

We find our true identity when we own and do less.

Sometimes, to discover what matters,
you have to get rid of everything that doesn't.

Courtney Carver

10. Journal Your Gratitude

The happiness of your life
depends on the quality of your thoughts.

Marcus Aurelius

I can stand in the middle of certain stores and pick up plenty of items that "spark joy." I'll bet you can too. But there's a ripple effect to retail therapy. When I look for joy in belongings, I always need the thrill of something new. Contentment is short-lived, because the next acquisition beckons. Then I need more space to store stuff, more time to take care of stuff, and more stuff to keep me interested once I've tired of the "old stuff."

If you've ever turned to shopping as a source of comfort and pleasure, I'd like to suggest a powerful replacement.

The practice of gratitude actually changes your brain in multiple positive ways.

Current research shows that gratitude increases serotonin levels, improving sleep, mood, and metabolism. Additionally, an attitude of thankfulness stimulates the production of dopamine, the neurotransmitter that's activated when something good unexpectedly happens. While acquiring a new pair of cute shoes can release a burst of dopamine, so can sitting down with a gratitude journal.

Dr. Alex Korb, author of *The Upward Spiral*, has discovered that even searching for things to be thankful for is beneficial. He writes:

> Trying to think of things you are grateful for forces you to focus on the positive aspects of your life. This simple act increases serotonin production in the anterior cingulate cortex.

His research looks at how this reverses symptoms of depression.

Unlike buying something new, the daily practice of gratitude will lead to long-lasting satisfaction. When you focus on what you are grateful for, you essentially crowd out your more negative thoughts. And since the brain constantly looks for things that prove what you already believe (it's called confirmation bias), by regularly scanning your life for what's good, your mind will start finding even more good things for you to appreciate.

Most of us have a lot to be happy about, even if we don't think so. And if we spend more time focusing on those good things – cultivating gratitude – we will feel happier. So gratefulness leads to happiness. It's an essential part of a quality life.

Unfortunately, many of us have the habit of focusing on our problems and woes. We spend a lot of time criticizing ourselves and finding fault with others. And just like gratitude, complaining and pessimism get easier with practice. So developing appreciation takes conscious effort. This is where a journal can be so beneficial.

Actually writing down what you're grateful for forces you to slow down, be more mindful, and really pay attention to the goodness in your life.

According to Robert Emmons and Michael McCullough, psychologists at the University of California, Davis, research shows that those who keep gratitude journals are not only more optimistic, but also experience more energy, enthusiasm, and emotional connection to others, while seeing more progress toward important personal goals. That's exciting!

So how do you journal your gratitude?

It's pretty easy to write a general list of items you're thankful for: nice weather, your spouse or a friend, your reliable car, a delicious omelet for breakfast. But if you take the time to get more specific, you'll create a stronger emotional response and a more powerful impact.

For example, I could list "I'm grateful for my husband Jon." And that's true, but it's very general and doesn't really inspire good feelings. But if I write

> I'm grateful for Jon because he encourages my writing, slows his pace so he can walk beside me, and makes me laugh. I'm grateful because we always have so much to talk about, and really enjoy spending time together, even after 35 years of marriage.

Now I've written something that gets to the heart of *why* I'm grateful for Jon, and it inspires me.

Eventually, just listing things you appreciate might become repetitious. Your kids, good health, seeing a good movie or a gorgeous sunset, a new pair of jeans that really fit.... Things like that are going to go on a gratitude list again and again. In one sense, that's great, because having continued good health and enjoying lots of beautiful sunsets is wonderful, and you should be grateful for those things. But in another sense it can start to feel uninspired, like you're just going through the motions, and you might be tempted to set aside your journaling practice.

But if you get more specific, and pay attention to the details that evoke good feelings or memories, you'll gain more benefit as you write.

Each time you mention that you appreciate nice weather, for example, your gratitude has probably been inspired for a different reason. Describe it. Later, if you reread parts of your journal, you'll experience those feelings again.

> I'm grateful for this windy fall day. The clouds are moving quickly, with occasional gleams of sunlight piercing through. I love the sound of wind in the trees and the freshness of the air. I'm thankful for the scent of approaching rain because we really need it!

Sometimes you might want to choose a focus for your gratitude. Consider:

- current or past relationships that have helped you
- wonderful experiences that you've had
- opportunities that have come or are coming your way
- things in the natural world that you love
- foods, items of clothing, movies, music, books, or other things you appreciate

Journaling your gratitude first thing in the morning will help you start your day with optimism and energy. It's been described as "a hit of caffeine for the soul." Making the practice part of your bedtime routine lets you reflect on good things that happened during the day, increasing your sense of calm and well-being and thus improving your sleep. Choose either time (or both). Just start today!

When you arise in the morning,
think of what a precious privilege it is
to be alive –
to breathe, to think, to enjoy, to love.

Marcus Aurelius

11. Kindness

Doing good makes you feel good.

Studies show that when we are kind to others we become happier, but that self-indulgence doesn't increase our feelings of well-being. Researchers found that the more generous and helpful people were, the more purposeful their lives felt. Knowing they were useful and needed made them happy.

This finding demonstrates the opposite of what advertisers want us to believe. As long as your basic needs are met, acquiring more won't make you happier. Your life won't improve if you buy the next hot item or luxury upgrade. But removing the excess and the busyness so you can pursue your life purpose has major benefits, for you and for others.

What does it mean to be kind? It's more than being "nice." Kindness means you've tried to understand another person, and you treat them the way you'd want to be treated. It's the Golden Rule: "Do to others what you would have them do to you." (Matthew 7:12, Holy Bible, New International Version)

Kindness may come easily when we're in a good mood and things are going well for us. It's harder when we're tired, or stressed, or disappointed, or when the person in front of us isn't behaving well. But that's when being kind can have the most powerful impact.

- When your child throws a tantrum, or wakes you up at 2:00 in the morning, be kind.
- When your partner is short-tempered after a stressful day, be kind.
- When your neighbor fails to pick up after his dog, state your case, but be kind.
- When your co-worker disagrees with you, share your opinion and reasons, but be kind.

These situations aren't pleasant, and kindness can be a difficult challenge. But you can choose to lighten the encounter, rather than making things worse. And it might open the door for better communication and a happier resolution.

20 Ways to Show Kindness

1. Smile and make eye contact.

Try leaving your phone in your bag so you can pay attention to the people around you.

2. Give a sincere compliment.

Of course you can admire someone's hair style or outfit, but it might mean more if you can praise their idea, creation, accomplishment, talent, or personality.

3. Yield.

Hold the door, let someone go ahead of you in line, and don't be a pushy motorist.

4. Greet your neighbor.

If you don't know him, introduce yourself.

5. Pick up trash.

It's easy to do as you walk around your neighborhood or through the park.

6. Plant a tree.

A tree provides beauty, shade, clean air, habitat for wildlife, improved soil and water conservation, and maybe even food. Planting one is a gift to future generations.

7. Write a note.

Share encouragement or appreciation.

8. Do a chore.

Complete a small job that rightfully belongs to your child, spouse, or co-worker. Don't say anything about it, just let them discover it done.

9. Give flowers.

Surprise your mother, your spouse, or another person dear to you with flowers or a special treat, "just because."

10. Invite.

Ask a friend, neighbor, or new acquaintance to join you for a meal, for coffee, or for a community event such as a concert or art show.

11. Make a date.

Arrange to spend some uninterrupted time with your partner, child, or other loved one, doing something that they like to do. Even if you don't care much for watching a football game, playing with wooden trains, or going to a quilt show, try to understand their interest, and enjoy the time you share with them.

12. Donate.

There are many opportunities, such as sponsoring a child in need, providing healthy staples to a local food pantry, or giving gently-used clothing and toys to a domestic violence shelter.

13. Give blood.

You'll help several people, and maybe even save a life.

14. Volunteer.

Pick a cause you care about, such as a homeless ministry, a senior center, a literacy program, an environmental group, a youth club, or an animal shelter, and give a few hours of your time and energy.

15. Purchase ethically.

Don't buy clothing brands that use sweatshops; avoid food and cosmetics from companies that mistreat animals.

16. Listen.

Give your full attention as someone tells you about their plans or their problems, without interrupting or criticizing. Ask questions, but don't try to tell them what you think they should do unless they ask your opinion.

17. Be inclusive.

Read or listen to alternate viewpoints. Try to understand another point of view, even if you disagree with it.

18. Keep your speech positive.

Don't indulge in gossip, but try to introduce a new subject. Don't respond in kind to someone's unpleasant words, but try to reply calmly. Ditch negative remarks and put your energy into fixing the problem. Radiate positive vibes rather than a toxic aura.

19. Give up perfectionism.

It's unreachable anyway! Don't be impossible to please. Be gracious about human error and shortcomings – including your own.

20. Forgive.

Carrying a grudge is hard and unpleasant work. Try to see the incident from the other person's point of view, and acknowledge your own part in the situation. Even if you believe most of the fault lies elsewhere, be the one to make the first move when you are calm enough to do so. Forgiveness doesn't mean you're condoning bad behavior. It simply allows you move on with a lighter emotional load.

One more thing about kindness: it seems to be catching. One person being kind can make others in a group more kind, which lifts everyone's spirits. It's a wonderful feedback loop.

So behave like the person you want to be. It really is the secret to happiness.

Minimalist Inspiration: *Jesus of Nazareth*

Born in about 4 BC into a working-class family, Jesus was a precocious student of the Jewish scriptures, impressing religious experts with his knowledge and understanding at age 12.

When he began his public career at approximately age 30, Jesus quickly gained fame and notoriety, followers and enemies. He was itinerant, never owning his own home, but staying in the homes of friends and supporters. When he died, he apparently possessed only the clothes he was wearing.

Jesus walked from place to place, teaching and helping people from all levels of society – rich and poor, Jewish and Roman, leaders and lepers. He was known to retreat from the crowds that followed him in order to pray, and also for his pithy, memorable stories about what God and His kingdom are like. Many of his stories displayed his deep understanding of human nature and his appreciation for the natural world.

In one of Jesus' most famous sermons, he reminded his hearers that earthly belongings are subject to theft and decay, but that spiritual treasures last forever. "Store up for yourselves treasures in heaven.... For where your treasure is, there your heart will be also." (Matthew 6:20-21, New International Version)

Another time, Jesus told a story about a rich man who tore down his barns in order to build bigger ones to house his excess goods. The man died that very night, having wasted his opportunity to find joy in pursuing God and being generous. Jesus summarized the lesson: "A man's life does not consist in the abundance of his possessions." (Luke 12:15, NIV)

12. Limits

His hair is sweaty and his face looks hot, but he doesn't slow down.

Up, across, down, run back, up, across, and down again. The sweat slips down his cheek, but his eyes are alight with eagerness and fun.

He's my 3-year-old grandson, and if I didn't call him over for a sip of lemonade now and again, he'd climb and slide and run around the play structure until he dropped from exhaustion. He has no idea of limits.

He may take only one bite of his grilled cheese, but he could eat "yummy wallypops" all day if I'd give them to him. He needs a bit of firmness at bath time or clean-up-toys time or bedtime, or he'd never be clean or rested until fatigue took over. He needs to be slowed down and reminded to wash his hands, or he'd just run out of the bathroom to play some more. He *can* be quiet, but rarely chooses that state. He needs the discipline of limits so he can stay healthy, comfortable, and socially acceptable!

Most of us grew up with parents or grandparents who loved us enough to set limits. Those limits protected and guided us, and even when we chafed at them, they were doing us good.

Eventually, we started to make our own decisions, and we began to test the limits. Whether we broke curfew, did a bit too much partying, or something else entirely, part of becoming an adult involved pushing on and breaking some of the boundaries we'd been taught to respect.

It was an education in decision-making and self-reliance. And most of us learned that some limits are necessary. Now we live within the law, we don't drink and drive, we pay our bills, we mind our manners and try to get along with people. We accept the limits that keep our society stable.

But there are other limits our culture expects us to ignore.

Our society labels us "consumers," and we're expected to buy. Buy to celebrate, buy to console. Buy to have what your friends have, or to be the first of your friends to own it. Buy to make your life easier, or more exciting, or to express yourself, or to realize your dreams. Buy because that thing you have is *so* last year, even though last year you were told it was the most wonderful, advanced thing in the world.

Even if you have no money, buy. It's on sale – buy two! Take this low interest loan, or get this credit card, or sign a contract and get the first month completely free!

Our society also labels us "busy." Busyness is a badge of honor. You're important, indispensable, and you don't want to miss out on anything. You're in the know, you retweet the hottest memes. Your kids are the brightest and the best and you push relentlessly. That Harvard acceptance letter or full-ride athletic scholarship is the route to happiness and respect. Go big or go home!

So we ignore limits.

Our big houses are stuffed to the gills. We buy everything we want, but are easily convinced we need more. We have debt – a lot of it. With our packed schedules, we're always running late, we're impatient, and we're constantly multi-tasking, which means we never fully pay attention to anything. We're sleep-deprived, anxious, and perpetually snacking.

When we collapse at the end of the day, we let Door Dash deliver food, binge watch TV, and scroll through social media. We don't listen, we don't converse. We don't really taste or smell. If we feel disconnected or lonely as a result, we stuff our feelings and buy something, or we get a prescription.

We have to stop blowing through the limits of our time, space, money, and energy.

We need to stop abusing our bodies and our spirits. We need to make room for creativity and kindness.

The reality is that it's impossible to have or do everything, and by pursuing the impossible we're throwing away what's really important.

Minimalism doesn't set limits, but it recognizes them.

Minimalism doesn't require you to have only 100 possessions, own a ten-item wardrobe, or live in a 300 square-foot tiny house. Minimalism helps you live with less clutter, less debt, less busyness, and less stress so you have room for what really matters to you. It helps you savor and enjoy the people, activities, and things that bring value to your life, while removing everything else. Minimalism can help you limit *yourself* in ways that bring joy, well-being, contentment, and freedom.

13. Memories, Not Mementos

Does that box of souvenirs really have sentimental value, or are you just caught in inertia or guilt?

When we have boxes full of stuff we never actually look at, it seems silly to claim we keep those things because of the wonderful memories they evoke. If that's the case, why aren't all of those things on display in our homes? Perhaps we need to consider whether the items truly mean as much as we think they do.

3 Reasons We Cling to Keepsakes

1. We feel guilt or obligation.

Your husband's Grannie, or your beloved aunt, gave it to you. It was important to her, so you feel you have to keep it, even though it's not your style and you have no use for it. Trust me, Grannie didn't intend to burden you or keep you trapped by guilt (and if she did, you have even less reason to honor her wishes). Even if it was a gift, *you have permission to let it go.* This is your home, and you have the right to make room for what matters to you.

2. We fear we'll lose memories if we lose the items.

You're not looking at or using items stashed in the back of a closet or in a box in the attic, so they're not actually available to jog any memories. Realize that the memory and emotion you value resides in your mind and heart – it doesn't exist in the item. If you're concerned that you'll forget, take a picture of the item before decluttering it.

3. The items represent a past accomplishment or phase of our lives.

If you have a box of newspaper clippings of your high school sports career, pick out the best ones and frame them for display, or make a scrapbook, and let the rest go. If you're too embarrassed to make a big deal of your teenage athletic accomplishments, maybe that's a sign the stuff isn't worth saving.

In fact, anything on a "glory wall" of memorabilia that's more than a decade old needs to be reconsidered, so that your display isn't sending the message that your best days are behind you. You don't want stagnation, you want movement and possibility. So take it all down and choose your favorites, replacing only half, or a quarter, or even just one representative item. Make space for new events and accomplishments.

Your past is important. The people you've known, the places you've been, the things you've learned have made you who you are today. But who you are has nothing to do with *possessions* and everything to do with *relationships* and *experiences*. Those are a part of you and won't disappear even if your house and everything in it burns to the ground. So you can be thankful for, yet move on from, past versions of yourself. **Who are you now?**

One carefully chosen keepsake is able to get the attention it deserves.

Buy a beautiful frame to display your favorite wedding photo, and sell or donate your gown (you certainly don't want to guilt your daughter into using it someday). You might not want your father's easel or all of his paintings, but you could keep and display the one you like best. Sell your aunt's doll collection if you don't care for it, but keep one of her Waterford vases if you'll appreciate and use it.

As you decide what to keep and what to release, you'll find that you enjoy your possessions more because each is unique. Your chosen items express your taste and values, rather than being a stale memorial to your past. And your memories are visible, so you'll savor them more often.

14. Non-Conform

As a teenager, I often argued with my mother, usually ending with a comment like "You just don't get me, Mom. I have to be myself!" Which is funny in retrospect, because I was always desperately trying to conform to what my peers were doing.

Even as adults, we continue to try to fit in. Look at a typical group of friends, and you'll often see similar hair styles and colors, similar clothes, similar manicures, similar phone cases, even similar gestures and vocal inflections.

If we're the one person in a group that doesn't conform, we tend to think that the others are "normal" and we aren't. We think there may be something wrong with us if we're too different from everyone else, and we worry that others will ignore or reject us if we aren't like them. That can feel scary.

85

But being "normal" is overrated. Sometimes we forget we don't have to do what everyone else is doing. Being unique, finding our own passions, remaining true to ourselves – that's the way to find happiness.

Minimalists aren't "normal."

We don't conform to our society, which pressures us to buy more, do more, hurry more, and work more. Our culture expects us to be mere consumers, but we know that fulfillment actually comes from being creative, kind, and useful. We know that when we're too busy chasing trivial things, we sacrifice our opportunity to find the things that really matter.

5 Ways to Non-Conform

1. Control the message.

The siren calls of our culture enter through our eyes and ears and take root in our minds if we don't limit their impact. We can watch less television, flip through fewer ads, and scroll through less social media. We can idolize fewer celebrities. As we begin to reduce the noise from outside, we're able to tune in to our own priorities, thoughts, and feelings.

2. Say no.

Agreeing to do things you don't want to do, or that you don't have time for, in order to please someone else or to keep from missing out is "normal." But this creates stress and resentment, and keeps you from doing things you actually want to do. Next time your heart says no, don't let your mouth say yes. You don't need an elaborate excuse or apology. Simply say, "No thanks!"

3. Don't keep it.

It's "normal" to keep everything because it was expensive, or because someone gave it to you, or because you might need it someday. Or maybe the kids will want it!

Minimalists clear out non-essentials to make room for the things that add value to our lives. By getting rid of the stuff that doesn't matter, we're left with only what we use and love.

- **If you're keeping something "just in case,"** realize that you're living with fear. Dig out some of the things that are buried in the back of your closet or in boxes in the garage, and admit that "just in case" means "never." When you free yourself of these items, you'll let go of some insecurity as well.

- **If you're keeping something because it was expensive**, realize you're feeling guilt. You spent a lot of money on something that wound up not meaning very much to you. But continuing to clean, store, maintain, and insure this item costs money, time, and attention. Let it go. You've paid enough.

- **If you're keeping something because it was a gift**, you don't have to. It has already served its purpose as a token from your loved one. And she probably didn't intend to burden you with something you don't like or can't use. In future, if you prefer not to receive physical gifts, have conversations with your near and dear to suggest getting together for a meal or a shared experience, or donating to a charity you both care about.

- **If you're keeping something because your kids might want it**, they don't. Just ask them! They don't want your clothes or most of your furniture or china or knickknacks, so go ahead and donate or sell them if you aren't using them. And if your adult children want their childhood memorabilia, give them a retrieval deadline. It's not your responsibility to store it for them.

4. Stop competing and comparing.

This is the "normal" way of our world, and it's destructive. If you find yourself doing this, ask yourself why you're so busy trying to impress everyone else that you're ignoring what makes you happy. If you're living at an impossible pace, ask yourself if abusing your body, brain, heart, and soul is worth it. If time spent on social media leaves you feeling jealous or dissatisfied, switch off your device. You can use that time to practice a hobby, exercise, be in nature, or meet face-to-face with a friend who will lift your spirits.

5. Think differently.

Most people don't change. They may complain about a situation, but they rarely change anything. But as the saying goes, "Reality doesn't change until we do."

Minimalism will lead you down a path that most people don't choose. They think it means lack and scarcity and deprivation. They question the choices of someone who might live with only one car or only six pairs of shoes, who keeps a flip phone instead of a smart phone, or who doesn't say yes to every available activity. It takes some determination and out-of-the-box thinking to be a non-conformist.

But minimalism is a tool that can help us find happiness by steering us in the direction of what we truly value. Minimalism lets us fill our lives with what is most important to us while forcing us to let go of what adds clutter and stress and steals our time, money, and attention. Living a minimalist life, a life of essentials, can help us find lasting rewards.

Two roads diverged in a wood, and I –
I took the one less traveled by,
and that has made all the difference.

Robert Frost

Minimalist Inspiration:
Walden

Published in 1854, *Walden* recounts Henry David Thoreau's two-year experiment in living with just the essentials. His hand-built, one-room cabin outside Concord, Massachusetts, was furnished with only a desk, a table, a bed, and three chairs: "one for solitude, two for friendship, three for society." He possessed little more than some clothes, a few cooking and eating implements, and writing materials.

Thoreau was part of a literary and philosophical movement called Transcendentalism, which began in New England in the 1830s. His mentor, Ralph Waldo Emerson, also wrote about the beliefs of this group, which included individualism, self-reliance and reverence for nature.

Walden is a detailed record of Thoreau's attempt to "live deliberately, to front only the essential facts of life." He dressed simply, ate sparingly, thought deeply, and lived by nature's rhythms rather than by the clock. He avoided commerce and the distractions of society, which he believed to be superficial and corrupting.

Walden is a classic that might inspire you to pare down, unplug, visit the wilderness, and ponder your purpose in the world.

15. One In, One Out

When decluttering, you identify the belongings you use the most and like the best, the items of the highest quality. You release things you don't like or use, and all of those multiples you've accumulated. Next, you find a home for each of the possessions you've chosen to keep.

Using containers such as boxes, bins, drawers, shelves, and closets, you put everything away. Your items will no longer pile up or drift around homeless; each has a place to belong. As you gain a clear idea of how much each container will hold, you are able to place limits on what you keep: how many shirts will hang in your closet, how many pairs of socks will go in their designated drawer, how many books will fit on your shelves, how many bins of holiday decorations will fit in the cupboard in the garage.

By respecting the physical limits of your space, the things you own can stay organized and uncluttered.

But minimalism isn't a choice you make once. It's a choice you make every day. Every day, you choose to maintain the limits you've established. You refuse junk mail, freebies, and "bargains." You propose gift-free holidays. You stop spending leisure time at the store or browsing online, and you start spending it at the park or the library, having coffee with a friend, crafting, journaling, exercising, or volunteering.

Of course you continue to shop, but you buy for need rather than want, for function rather than diversion. And when you bring something new into your home, you make a like-for-like trade: a book for a book, a sweater for a sweater, a couch for a couch.

When a new one comes in, an old one goes out.

When you come home from back-to-school shopping, your kids should get rid of as many old clothes as they add to their closets. When you bring home new shoes, an old pair must go. New towels, cookware, lamps, or phones must replace what's already there.

This trade-off maintains balance in your home so that it never again becomes overstuffed.

As you practice the one in, one out technique, it becomes a natural part of the way your family operates. But you must also practice thinking before you buy. Mindfulness needs to be an element of every shopping trip you take.

5 Questions to Ask Before a Purchase

1. Does it satisfy a need?

Make sure it's a true need, not a momentary sense of boredom, sadness, worry, or "Oooh, *that's* cute!" This doesn't mean that every purchase must be drab or utilitarian. Those red sandals might be perfect if they're of high quality, fit well, go with more than one outfit, and are replacing something else.

2. Does it offer value?

The thing you're about to buy should appear well-made and able to perform the function you need from it. If a low price is its only enticement, don't buy it.

3. Does it provide versatility?

When possible, avoid buying specialty or single-task items. Favor items that can be useful in several ways, like stemless tumblers instead of multiple types of drinking glasses, or a simply-styled dress that can be modified with jewelry, a scarf, a belt, or a jacket.

4. Is it the result of a careful decision?

Impulse buying almost always generates clutter. Notice what you want to buy, and tell yourself that if you still want it in seven days you can come back and buy it guilt-free. Do you even remember it a week later? Or does your sudden "need" dissipate during that time?

5. Does it work right now?

Don't buy décor for a house you hope to own "someday." Don't buy something telling yourself you'll lose weight and it will be perfect. New clothes must fit today. Don't buy shoes you hope will stretch out enough to become comfortable. They won't.

This kind of restraint may not come naturally – it's a rare and wonderful thing in this age of excess! But it's worth practicing, not just because it keeps us free of clutter, debt, and stress, but because it conserves our planet's resources, creates less waste, and lets us (and our children) learn to value creativity, generosity, and relationships over stuff.

We make a living by what we get,
but we make a life by what we give.

Winston Churchill

16. Preserve Public Works

Some of our greatest treasures are things we don't own – and never can:

- the beauties of nature, music, and art
- the comfort of good relationships
- the incredible riches of good health and an active mind

Think of the value in public works: Libraries, public parks, the Golden Gate Bridge, highways and road maintenance crews, law enforcement, fire protection, water treatment and garbage removal, public schools and colleges, government-supported scientific and medical research, health departments.

These good things can be available to everyone. Yes, they're supported by property taxes, gasoline taxes, and sales taxes, but those are paid by everyone proportionally. The rich pay more because they buy and travel more, and their property is more valuable. The poor pay less for all the same reasons. But everybody contributes, so that everybody can benefit.

About public schools, US President John Adams wrote, "The whole people must take upon themselves the education of the whole people and be willing to bear the expenses of it." Public schools not only provide access to education, but opportunities for all children. While they are not perfect, in an all-private-school world the wealthy would almost always fare better than everyone else. There's also evidence that schools would be more segregated, not just by race, but by special needs. Public schools, already providing excellent services to many children, could be even more successful if everyone recognized their stake in the outcome.

Public parks have been called "our open-air living rooms." They are a vital part of everyday life, especially in cities. Playgrounds, picnic spaces, sports facilities, and hiking trails are invaluable resources, but so are mature trees and shrubs, which clean the air and refresh our spirits. Public gardens and memorials are rejuvenating and instructive. And then there are all the beautiful state and national parks, from beaches to ancient redwood groves to Yosemite's granite domes and waterfalls, the Grand Canyon, and, oldest of all, Yellowstone. We share these wonderful parks with visitors from all over the world.

Public spaces are literally common ground. They strengthen our sense of community and let us gather together face to face. When all interaction shifts to impersonal forums like talk radio or web sites, we splinter into smaller, more insulated groups.

Democracy loses its meaning if citizens don't have any shared spaces and services.

In a culture that continues to become more and more commercialized, where money and property are being concentrated in fewer and fewer hands (think, for example, of how much of all media is now controlled by Disney), public spaces and services that are available to all citizens have become an even greater asset.

Defunding public libraries, parks, museums, and transportation services might save local governments some money, but at what cost to the quality of life for the people and the community?

Libraries, for example, have shown that they are highly adaptable, changing to reflect new technology and community needs. Libraries offer not only print books, e-books, music, movies, and games that can be freely borrowed, but provide computers and internet access. There are story times and summer reading clubs for children, adult literacy, ESL, and citizenship classes, and resources for job seekers and entrepreneurs. Some provide maker spaces and meeting spaces, even concert spaces that can be used free of charge. Libraries are safe, welcoming places where community members can meet, learn, and socialize. They charge no entrance or user fees, which is the beauty, and the challenge, of the public library.

Privatizing everything means commercializing it.

- We don't want public libraries to be replaced by Amazon bookstores (as advocated by an opinion piece in *Forbes* magazine).
- We don't want public schools to be replaced by for-profit training centers.
- We don't want public parks to be replaced by Six Flags or McDonald's play areas.
- We don't want all gardens to be walled off like private golf courses.
- We don't want to rely on bottled water because city water treatment plants have been shuttered.
- We don't want to hire security because there are no more police.
- We don't want our children to be forced into debt because community colleges and state universities have disappeared.
- And we *definitely* don't want irreplaceable natural wonders to be lost to exploitation and "development."

Because of public works, we don't sacrifice quality of life if we own less. Minimalists celebrate public works.

We may "buy" these treasures when we pay taxes, but they don't become our personal property.   And because we join with everyone else in paying for them, we create so much more than we ever could on our own.   Rugged individualism is all very well, but life is richer when we share.

The miracle is this:
the more we share, the more we have.

Leonard Nimoy

17. Quality Over Quantity

We took our 3-year-old grandson to the park earlier this summer. He had one toy truck with him – a very sturdy plastic dump truck. That little truck was his constant companion for two hours, and when his mama put him in the car seat to go home, he was still cradling it.

He has many toy cars and trucks of all sizes at home, and several at our house too. But when there's only one to play with, that one is cherished. It almost takes on a personality as he tells stories about what that toy can do. It can go to the beach, play in the sand, play in the bathtub, hold water, dump rocks, and roll down the slide to be caught at the bottom – it's Super Truck!

I have one pair of fit-over sunglasses given to me by my son. They're oversized, designed to be worn over my prescription bifocals, and I love them because I can see near or far while I'm wearing them. They have wide arms which incorporate a small area of tinted lens, so even my peripheral vision is protected from UV glare. They're lightweight and scratch resistant, and I take very good care of them even though they aren't that expensive to replace.

Just because they aren't expensive doesn't mean I should treat them like junk.

In fact, if I treat them like a quality item, they'll last for a long time, and I'll enjoy tons of use from just one pair. Just like my grandson's dump truck. Or our antique dresser. Or my leather wallet. Or my versatile kitchen utility knife. Or our one reliable, gas-efficient car.

Our consumer society constantly badgers us to replace or upgrade our possessions. The average American buys a new car every few years and considers furniture to be a short-term style statement rather than a long-term investment.

As for sunglasses, clothes, accessories, kitchenware, phones, and more – those seem to be considered completely expendable, bought with the idea that you'll lose them quickly, or tire of them and want something different when you're bored or the season changes.

But if we treat things like they're valuable, we'll appreciate them more and extend their usable life. We'll be more satisfied with what we own. We'll shop less and throw less away.

We waste so much because we're not expected to care for our belongings. From fast food and fast fashion to continually upgraded devices, we consume more and more and toss things away for something new because none of what we buy has any value. We have no reason to care for something that is only of the moment and never meant to last.

Minimalism doesn't mean we become reckless with our possessions. As we declutter, we don't wastefully and thoughtlessly throw everything away. That's not minimalism – that's irresponsibility.

Minimalism has the opposite effect. It requires us to be increasingly thoughtful about the things we own. And if something is worth owning, it's worth buying a quality item that will serve its purpose for a long time.

When we own quality items and take good care of them, we don't replace them so often. We make them last. Choosing quality and taking care reduces waste, clutter, and dissatisfaction. It's the cure for consumerism, and a big win for our wallets and the environment.

How well are you caring for the things you own?

- Have you done routine maintenance on your car? Is it reasonably clean and clutter-free?

- Do you take care of repairs and maintenance around your home (fix the leak, clean the spot on the rug, wash the windows and blinds, clear out the roof gutters, etc.)?

- Do you own clothing worth caring for, and do you take care (fold it/hang it up when you're not wearing it, sew on missing buttons, treat stains, hand wash as necessary, etc.)?

- Do you clean your shoes and treat the leather?

- Do you keep your furniture dusted and polished?

- Do you vacuum upholstery, pillows, and mattresses occasionally (more often if you have pets)?

- Do you use all of your dishes and cooking implements, or are they just sitting in cupboards gathering dust?

- Have you cleaned your oven lately? Or your refrigerator?

- Do you back up your computer files and keep crumbs and dust off the keyboard and screen?

- Do you actually read the books, water and care for the plants, look at the pictures, and enjoy your art and other decorative objects, or are they just paperweights and dust catchers?

- Do you keep up with routine medical tests, eye exams, and dental care?

- Are you sleeping, exercising, hydrating, eating plenty of fruits and vegetables, and limiting highly processed foods?

- Are you learning, creating, and doing good in the world, or do you merely consume it?

Quality is never an accident.
It is always the result of intelligent effort.

John Ruskin

Minimalist Inspiration:
Design

Your home is the base that supports you. It should be a peaceful haven, comfortable for family and friends, not weighed down by cluttered rooms and overstuffed furnishings. Be inspired by Shaker, Desert, Scandinavian, or Japanese design.

The Shakers, a religious sect active in 18th and 19th century America, were known for their simplicity and craftsmanship. Their beautiful wooden furniture is utilitarian and unadorned, yet classically elegant. Shaker-style cabinets are still popular in kitchens today, a testament to their timeless design. Peg rails are used to hang clothing, towels, brooms, baskets, cookware, and more, keeping floors and counters clutter-free. Soft white walls, lots of windows, and a neutral palette of tan, gray, and muted blue or green are all in keeping with the style.

Modern desert décor, like the landscape, is spare and earthy. Against a backdrop of crisp white walls, cool tile floors, and neutral modern furniture, a kilim or Navajo rug adds brightness and pattern, mixing with aged leather, rustic baskets, and touches of wrought iron and gold. Vibrant colors such as orange, navy, cocoa, and turquoise are perfect accents. Natural elements might include a live edge table or geode bookends. Pots of succulents, a snake plant, a Mexican ponytail palm, or a vase of eucalyptus cuttings add life and greenery.

Scandinavian style is known for pale interiors which maximize natural light. Warm gray walls and blonde wood floors create a sense of space, providing a serene backdrop for sleek modern furniture. A few accessories add color, often in subtle shades of blush pink or ice blue, although brights like lemon yellow are also popular. Warmth and texture come from sheepskin throws, shag rugs, and down bedding. Candles and mirrors add and reflect light, and lush plants such as Boston fern or English ivy bring nature indoors.

Japanese design is pared down and simple. It incorporates streamlined storage and square, low-slung furniture to make rooms look and feel spacious. Features include lots of wood and natural light, woven sea grass rugs, translucent doors and screens (shoji), and a shoe rack near the front door. An alcove (tokonoma) creates a focal point with a painted scroll and perhaps an orchid or a jade plant bonsai. Homes are often surrounded by a small walled garden of gravel, rocks, a pond, and carefully chosen plants and trees.

Browse online to see which style appeals to you, but instead of running out to buy new things, use the ideas you see to work with what you have. Decluttering plus design inspiration can make your home a place you love to be.

18. Rethink Leisure

Lately, news headlines have been proclaiming that "Sitting Is the New Smoking." In the sense that they're both linked to a lot of health threats, then yes, sitting and smoking do have a lot in common.

Here's where they *aren't* alike: **Smoking is much less widespread.** A growing number of cities, states, and countries have enacted laws that ban smoking in all work and public places, including restaurants and bars. The Centers for Disease Control reports that the number of smokers in the US has fallen to a record low.

But sitting is far more acceptable. In fact, we all do more of it than ever. Most of us have jobs that require little or no physical exertion. We might do a little standing, lifting, and walking around, but mostly we sit.

When we go home, we sit some more, watching hours of TV, streaming services, or YouTube, and scrolling on Facebook, Instagram, and other social media.

The thing that Americans do most often with their free time is not cooking or hiking or pursuing a hobby. **Americans sit and watch screens.** I have the same bad habit.

All this sitting contributes to poor health and fitness. As we spend more time sitting, we're more likely to experience:

- **Obesity.**

   Research has found that adults who spend more time sitting have a higher body mass index and waist size. Not only are we not using that time to move more and burn more calories, but we tend to eat when we're sitting. And when we're idly watching TV, we're more likely to eat junk food than any healthier alternatives.

- **Disease.**

   Studies show that for each additional hour spent watching TV, we have a 26% higher chance of developing metabolic syndrome, which can lead to diabetes and heart disease. Researchers have also found links between hours spent sitting and several types of cancer.

- **Early death.**

  Other studies show that people who sit for more hours every day have a higher risk of dying than those who spend fewer hours seated. Even if those people who sat longer were physically active during other times of the day, they had a higher risk of dying.

Did you catch that last part? **Even if you exercise every day, sitting around too much is harmful to your health.** Spending time at the gym doesn't erase the effects of a mostly sedentary life.

Isn't it odd that we deem the term "sitting room" as quaint? Today we have *living* rooms, right? Or do we? While we refer to the space in our homes where we spend most of our leisure time as the "living room," the truth is that it has become a sitting-down room.

The way I use my living room might be keeping me from looking and feeling my best.

We definitely don't want to be typical Americans in this area, do we? How can we turn our living rooms, family rooms, dens, man caves, and she sheds from places where we sit to places where we relax healthfully?

5 Ways to Keep Your Living Room from Making You Sick

1. Spend less time in the room.

Decide that one night a week will involve a family outing. Visit a neighborhood park, go on a bike ride, go bowling or to the roller rink, take a family trip to the gym, or simply take a long evening walk.

2. Control snacking.

Eating after dinner is especially bad if you want to control your weight. It's much better to eat a healthy, filling meal than it is to snack later. And many of us eat when we're bored, or because it's a habit to nosh on fatty chips, cookies, or candy when focused on a screen. If you think you're hungry, drink some water or tea, since we sometimes mistake thirst for hunger. If you need more, try one of these options:

- An apple, an orange, or a handful of grapes
- Celery with a little nut butter
- Carrot sticks with some hummus
- A serving of low-fat cottage cheese or plain Greek yogurt with berries
- One stick of string cheese
- A hard-boiled egg
- A handful of raw or dry roasted nuts
- Air-popped popcorn

3. Use some old workout videos.

Vow that for every hour you're in front of a screen, you'll spend 15 minutes working out. You don't even need the video if you walk around the block once every hour, or do jumping jacks, squat kicks, leg raises, push-ups, or even some house cleaning or decluttering during every commercial break.

4. Plan a "no electronics" night.

One night a week, leave the TV, computer, phones, and tablets off. Use your living room to play charades, Simon Says (funny when adults play too!), Twister, or balloon volleyball. Build a blanket fort. Or expand your living space by playing tag in and around the house. Let your body and brain take a break from electronic stimulation.

5. Do more jobs without labor-saving devices.

As we spend more time sitting in front of screens, we spend less time actively doing household chores. So get rid of the Roomba and push a vacuum cleaner. Donate the bread machine and bring back kneading. Hand-wash your dishes and your car. Sell your riding mower and buy a human-powered push mower. Instead of a leaf blower, use a rake. Instead of hiring the neighbor kid to shovel snow or pull weeds, do it yourself (and involve your own kids).

Make sure your leisure time is actually doing you good!

19. Single-task

Many of us have (or had) jobs that require juggling two or three tasks at a time while continuing to be available to bosses or clients. Or we meet the needs of two or three young children while managing household tasks and honoring volunteer commitments.

It can be crazy. Rushed and overwhelmed, you repeatedly lose focus and have to backtrack, trying to remember where you left off. You can't give your full attention to one thing at a time, so everything takes longer, and any minor holdup can become a major meltdown.

Before you know it, the day is over and you feel like you did nothing well. Perhaps you commute, switching your attention between driving, making phone calls, and trying to get through that audio book everyone's talking about.

You're in a hurry, and mentally review your to-do list: pick up your kid at school, get her to dance class, run to the post office and the grocery store, pick her up again, drive home fast to let the dog out before he has an accident you'll have to clean up, and either cook something for dinner or decide which takeout food everyone wants. Answer some texts and emails, get your kid into bed, run over logistics for tomorrow with your spouse, and fall onto the couch with your cell phone and the TV remote. Maybe you can relax before you fall asleep.

Time, the finite minutes of your life, slips away. Once it passes, it's gone forever.

We are all given the same 24 hours. We're told we can accomplish more if we just learn to multi-task more efficiently. But if our attention is diffused, we actually accomplish less while feeling more frazzled.

When you decide to multi-task, you're actually inviting interruption and distraction. What we call multi-tasking is really our brains frantically switching back and forth.

Many people think they're skilled at multi-tasking, but the brain doesn't actually work that way. Our brains have to choose which information to process. For example, if you listen to speech, your visual cortex becomes less active, and vice versa. When you talk on the phone to your mother and work on your computer at the same time, you literally hear less of what Mom is saying.

Researchers at Stanford University found that multi-tasking is less productive than doing one thing at a time. Multi-tasking takes more energy, so even simple tasks take longer than they should. People who are regularly bombarded with several streams of information cannot pay attention, organize their thoughts, filter out irrelevancies, recall important information, or even switch between tasks as smoothly.

So no, you can't actually have a conversation while scrolling through social media.

Even more disturbing, a study at the University of London showed that multi-taskers experience IQ score declines similar to someone who has smoked marijuana or stayed up all night. Their scores resembled those of an 8-year-old child.

In fact, multi-tasking may cause or indicate brain damage. Research completed at the University of Sussex found that high multi-taskers (in this case, people who spend a lot of time texting while watching TV or answering email while talking on the phone) had less brain density in the anterior cingulate cortex, a region responsible for empathy and emotional control.

Tell me how people with less empathy and emotional control make good co-workers, marriage partners, parents, or neighbors!

4 Ways to Find Clarity

1. Cut the buzz.

Many of us live and work with the constant background noise of radio, TV, or traffic. Especially when the sounds are those of people talking, such as with news, ads, or co-workers, there is a constant drag on our brain's ability to focus. Question your need for constant stimulation, and consider removing these noises if you can, since research shows that most people are more productive when working in silence. If you feel you must have accompaniment, choose purely instrumental music.

2. Practice single-tasking.

Bouncing between tasks may seem to relieve boredom, but it drains our cognitive abilities. Stick with one item until completion if you can. If attention starts to wane, you can switch to a new task, but take a moment to leave yourself a note about where you were with the first one. Then give the new task your full attention, again for as long as you can. As you practice single-tasking, you'll stretch your attention span, develop sharper focus, and access greater creativity.

3. Identify your elephants.

Most people have a long to-do list and choose the easiest tasks first so they can have the satisfaction of crossing something off the list. The difficult jobs get pushed until later when the brain is tired. But cognitive neuroscientist Sandra Chapman suggests focusing on your two "elephants" when creating your to-do list.

These are the most important tasks for the day, the ones to which you want to give your best efforts and attention. If time allows, you can move on to other tasks.

4. Close your door.

In the "old days," people did this when they really needed to concentrate. You need to figuratively close your door on electronic distractions if you want to be productive and creative, and you cannot continually respond to texts or emails if you want to nurture relationships. Remove text alerts from your phone, and put it in your bag or another room. Close browser tabs and remove email alerts from your computer. Check texts, voice mail, and email only at specific times during the day.

It's ironic that we get more done when we slow down.

When we try to multi-task, we're less productive, more stressed, and ultimately less happy. Give your attention to things that really matter. Focus on your priorities and let the rest go without guilt.

> ### Never half-ass two things.
> ### Whole-ass one thing.
>
> Ron Swanson on *Parks and Recreation*

20. Travel Light

When we travel, we have the perfect opportunity to try a different lifestyle.

Packing for travel is a bit like decluttering. You have to consider carefully which clothes you'll need, which toiletries and accessories. Maybe you make a list. As you pack, you might think of a few additional items it would be nice to have, just in case. But you're still limiting your choices – you're only going to take a fraction of your possessions, after all.

As you roll your suitcase out the door, are you full of excitement and anticipation, or are you worried that you've forgotten something important? Hopefully, you let that sense of freedom take over and realize that you'll probably do just fine with what you have. You know you packed the *really* important stuff, because those things were on your list.

118

When you arrive at your destination, you're greeted by a clean, uncluttered hotel room with its freshly made bed. You have no desire to turn on the TV for distraction, like you might do at home, because the outside world beckons. You unpack quickly, but you're no longer worrying about the things you brought with you. As you step out the door, you feel light on your feet, interested to see what lies around the corner, and already paying attention to the details of your new location. You don't have the usual chores or work responsibilities weighing you down, so you have plenty of time to explore.

When we carry only the essentials, we practice minimalism.

What does your suitcase say about you? Mine used to say, "I'm insecure and fearful I won't have enough, so I've stuffed in as much as possible." Sometimes it said, "I'm desperate to impress the people I'm going to see." Today, I think it says "I'm simple, comfortable, and confident." That's because I've learned to pack lightly.

When you travel with more than you really need, you weigh yourself down. You're slower, less flexible, and have more to think about and manage. But when you live for a week with a small suitcase of belongings, you're reminded of how little you actually require. You also get a clear sense of which clothes fit well, flatter your body and your coloring, and are comfortable and easy-care, since that's probably what has seen the most use.

On your next trip, pack the clothes and other items you think you need, and then remove half of them. Leave the "just in case" items at home. Notice how light you feel when walking through the airport, unpacking at the hotel, and exploring your surroundings without worrying about all of your stuff.

When we're faced with new places and experiences, we're motivated to be mindful.

But I'm sure you've seen the opposite: people at a beautiful beach or an ancient monument, staring at their phones, seemingly checking email. Don't you want to say, "You're missing it. Don't miss it!"

I read recently that it's hard to get close to the Leaning Tower of Pisa, or to see it properly, because hundreds of people are around it, pretending to push it for their Instagram posts. Really? Does every single person who goes to Pisa need that photo? When you're taking that, you're not even looking at the tower you came to see!

Actually, scientists now think that taking a photo shorts out the brain's ability to store a memory. The first step to forming a lasting memory is to pay attention. By paying attention to getting a great photo, our brains get the message that we don't have to remember the event, since we're "exporting" that memory to the camera. Our brains don't create the connections necessary to send the memory of what we're seeing to long-term storage.

And if we're so focused on photos and visuals, we're more likely to ignore other stimuli around us. What gets ignored does not get remembered. When we're hunting for the perfect Facebook shot, we're not listening, we're not smelling, we're not mindful of the beautiful, complex details that make up the moment. We're actually limiting our experience when we take too many photos.

Photos do serve as memory cues, but they don't tell the whole story. Put your camera down, fully participate in the real life of your trip, and choose a few good postcards on which to write notes about all of the details you savored. These will be your best souvenirs.

When we're free of our normal obligations and distractions, we experience time affluence.

Time affluence is the feeling that you have enough time for the activities that you care about. There are studies showing that people who commit to maintaining some unscheduled time tend to be happier overall than those who don't, probably because being over-scheduled makes us feel anxious, overworked, and out of control.

Americans seem to be suspicious of unscheduled time. Even on vacation we get so worried that we're going to miss something, we rush from here to there, making ourselves nervous and impatient. We're so focused on our itinerary that we may wind up missing the experience of being in a new place – not the tourist destination that we're determined to cross off a bucket list, but the *actual* place. The streets, the houses, the shops, the sky, the scents, the sounds, and most of all, the people.

Consider scheduling just one must-see destination per day, and don't rush through anything. Leave time for serendipity so you can explore off the beaten path. It's true, you might not visit every single thing that's available (that's probably impossible anyway). But what you *do* experience will be deeper, more detailed and memorable. And you'll come home feeling like you really got away.

I get ideas about what's essential
when packing my suitcase.

Diane von Furstenberg

21. Unplug

I love the internet. I couldn't have a blog without it, nor could I connect via Facebook, Instagram, or email. The internet makes extensive research easier and opens up tons of news and entertainment options.

But we need to get away from the internet sometimes. It's open 24/7/365, and we're not. We can't be. We need to take breaks from our phones and computers so we can enjoy real life.

And when we return, our computers and phones need to be tools we control, not addictions that control us.

Courtney Carver, author of *Soulful Simplicity*, has made it a goal to unplug one day a week. That's 52 days a year "to trade what's online for what's right in front of us."

4 Steps to an Internet Intermission

1. Schedule it.

Pick a 24-hour block that works for you. It might be a certain day (like Sunday), or it might straddle two days (like Friday after work until Saturday evening).

2. Prepare for it.

Tell friends and family when you'll be offline. If you usually take notes on your phone, keep a small notebook or some Post-its handy. If your phone is your alarm clock, consider using a regular alarm clock.

3. Rethink excuses.

If you're thinking "No way" or "Easier said than done," keep thinking. Challenge yourself. Maybe 24 hours seems like a long time, but you won't know if you don't try. Examine your feelings after the break. Were there certain times you particularly missed the internet? Why was that? Did you get bored? Did you pay more attention to the people around you? Did you use your senses more, or have more creative ideas? Whatever your experience, think about it and then make a decision about what works best for you.

4. Plan shorter breaks.

Even if you decide 24 hours is too long, you can still practice regular, shorter breaks. Commit to no internet before a certain time each morning or after a certain time in the evening. Alternatively, give yourself an hour in the morning and an hour in the evening to be on the internet, and take the rest of the day off. Make unplugging work for you.

Exchange a screen for fresh air, news for laughter, and texts for talking face-to-face.

On regular days when you're online, consider how you're using this wonderful tool. Is it helping you learn more, get more done, and meet the needs of friends and clients? Or is it a time suck that enables gossip, comparisons, discontent, and bad feelings? **Does the way you use it make it a blessing or a curse?**

On social media, consider "friending" only those who are actually your friends. Use it as a means to connect with them, not as a way to reach a certain number that makes you feel popular or to achieve a certain rating. While you're at it, limit groups and people you follow to what truly adds value to your life.

Think carefully about how you will use your devices to aid in decluttering. It's a good idea to digitize photos, music, movies, books, and important papers to reduce clutter. But even digital space can be cluttered if you can't find a file or an app because of other stuff that obscures it.

You don't want to waste time searching for your keys, the scissors, or your favorite earrings among piles of clutter and excess, and you don't want to search for digital content either. Delete what you no longer use, and sort everything else into descriptively-named folders. Make it a habit to organize new acquisitions.

Just because you can remove shelves full of books, movies, or CDs by using a digital device doesn't mean you should continue to acquire everything that catches your eye. Impulse buying is still a budget-buster, even if the purchase doesn't take physical space. And controlling that impulse is a key to becoming intentional about your life.

Minimalism is about removing things that crowd out what's important to you, not just about making those things smaller or more portable.

Just as owning ten of anything doesn't make you ten times happier, having fewer possessions, physical or digital, doesn't make you less happy. Regina Wong, author of *Make Space: A Minimalist's Guide to the Good and the Extraordinary*, says that "having less, but having the right stuff, can deliver more fulfillment."

Less, but better. It's a good mantra for everything, including all things digital.

22. Voluntary Simplicity

A common misconception about minimalism is that if you have or earn very little, you must be a minimalist. In fact, as you've progressed in your minimalist journey, some well-meaning acquaintances may have asked if you were having financial difficulties, since that's the only reason they can imagine that you would choose to own and buy less.

But minimalism isn't about trying to get by with as little as possible (though you might explore those limits as an interesting experiment). It's not about being cheap, and it's not meant to glorify or romanticize real poverty.

Multiple studies show that the rich people of the world (that includes us!) are not as happy as one might expect, given their level of comfort and opportunity.

A life of materialism can create feelings of loneliness, depression, and anxiety. It consumes huge quantities of natural resources, creates pollution, and makes us less likely to share with those in need. It turns out that too much stuff, too much busyness, too much distraction, too much food, and too much debt is a ruinous combination.

Minimalism means that you own what feels right for you, what you need and what you enjoy, without having excess that makes your life more complicated than you would like. If you regularly have trouble finding the things you need because of clutter, if your schedule is so packed you're constantly impatient and on edge, if you have no funds for an emergency or a good cause, or if you're deep in debt but just can't stop shopping, then you're not living a life that meets your needs. In that situation, you're probably not as happy as you could be.

In contrast, a minimalist removes the things that weigh her down, or keep her too busy, or take energy and money away from things she'd rather be doing. The choice is deliberate, purposeful, intentional. It's *voluntary* simplicity.

You can start small. Remove clutter from your work area, and notice that you can focus more easily and streamline your productivity, resulting in less stress. Remove clutter from your kitchen, and notice that it's easier to prepare meals and even eat more healthfully. Remove clutter from your calendar, and notice that you're less rushed while enjoying your chosen activities more. The results can ripple outward from wherever you start.

Minimalism has plenty of luxuries, they're just different luxuries from the ones most people choose.

Minimalism puts the emphasis on things that money can't buy. It doesn't require you to live in a 300-square-foot tiny house with a ten-item wardrobe. Minimalism's only guideline is **LESS:** less clutter, less debt, less busyness, and less stress. You decide what level of **LESS** will allow you to more effectively enjoy the people, activities, and things that bring value to your life.

Voluntary Simplicity:
a manner of living that is outwardly simple
and inwardly rich –
a deliberate choice to live with less
in the belief that more life
will be returned to us in the process.

Duane Elgin

129

Minimalist Inspiration:
Children's Literature

If more of us valued food and cheer and song
above hoarded gold,
it would be a merrier world.

J. R. R. Tolkien *The Hobbit*

When we get rid of the excess, we're left with the things that are truly valuable.

∅

I declare! Sometimes it seems to me
that every time a new piece of machinery
comes into the door
some of our wits fly out at the window!

Dorothy Canfield Fisher *Understood Betsy*

Our devices are useful tools, but bad masters. When we let them steal our time, attention, motivation, and imagination, we make ourselves less than human. The best computer ever invented is the human brain. Time away from technology to actually live our lives is essential.

It isn't the great big pleasures that
count the most;
it's making a great deal out of the little ones.

Jean Webster *Daddy Long-Legs*

We tend to live for the big events and accomplishments, but most of life doesn't happen on the high points. Life's value is in the little moments: daily choices, encounters, and activities. Don't miss any of it while thinking about the next big thing.

∅

… it does seem as if the more one gets
the more one wants….

Louisa May Alcott *Little Women*

Contentment is not the fulfillment of what we want, but the realization of how much we already have.

∅

Where you tend a rose, my lad,
a thistle cannot grow.

Frances Hodgson Burnett *The Secret Garden*

When you focus on gratitude, you crowd out negative thoughts.

23. Wear a Capsule Wardrobe

I'm sure you've seen Pinterest photos of beautifully curated closets and capsule wardrobes. Maybe you long for one yourself, but think it's impossible or too restrictive.

It's a modern consumer belief that we need a huge wardrobe to be "interesting." Of course you want to be appropriately dressed, and why not wear attractive clothes that flatter your body type and coloring? But none of that demands a huge quantity of clothing. Limits encourage creativity, and a smaller closet isn't necessarily boring.

In the 1940s the average person owned 36 items of clothing. Today the average consumer has 120 items, **with 80% going unworn.** This tells me several things:

- 20% of what's in the average closet (that's 24 pieces of clothing) may be an adequate wardrobe.

- We hang on to clothes that haven't fit for years and (if we're honest) will never fit again. Even if we could wear them, they'd be out of style. These clothes mock us and wreck our confidence.

- We hang on to clothes that we will never wear again: prom dresses, concert tee shirts, cheerleader uniforms. These souvenirs crowd our closets, waste our time, and keep us from concentrating on who we are *now*.

- We're quite obviously *addicted* to shopping, whether we need anything or not. We're worse than any 3-year-old nagging for a new toy!

I remember my mother talking about the best-dressed woman in the downtown San Francisco firm where Mom worked before I was born. She was secretary to the president of the company. This lady apparently owned five high-quality, beautifully tailored dresses for work, and rotated through them each week. Navy, burgundy, emerald, gray, purple. The same dress, just a different color. A different belt, scarf, or perhaps a cardigan or piece of jewelry would introduce subtle variety. Apparently, everyone agreed this woman always looked elegant and powerful.

She was interesting; her clothes were clothes.

We need clothing, but it should never be the most remarkable thing about us.

You may already own the core of a great capsule wardrobe, once you've decluttered the 80% that doesn't fit, that you never wear, that's no longer in good shape, or that doesn't go with anything else in your closet.

There are two secrets to a minimalist wardrobe: **separates and color**. A wardrobe built on separates such as skirts, trousers, jeans, tees, blouses, cardigans, and jackets, in a few coordinating colors, allows all of the pieces to be mixed and matched into a maximum number of wearable outfits.

If you need a clue to what will work best for you, consider pieces you already own that make you feel attractive and confident. Notice styling and details that these items share. You probably already have a few favorite colors you wear most often because you like the way you look in them. Intentionally wearing fewer colors also means you need fewer accessories (shoes, belts, handbags, etc.)

If you work in an office or a classroom, as I used to do, you'll want outfits that are professional yet comfortable. I used to own three similar skirts (navy, taupe, burgundy) and two trousers (black, charcoal). With about eight shirts or blouses and four cardigans or jackets, I could mix and match to create at least two dozen outfits, more than enough for a month of work days without an exact repeat.

Just one is a concept that can be applied to certain areas of your wardrobe. Sometimes one is enough: one swimsuit, one formal dress, one winter coat, one leather belt, one pair of sneakers, one handbag. Consider owning just one of some things, based on your occupation, lifestyle, and climate.

For some, shopping for clothes is a habit, something they do with certain friends or when they're bored. Become aware of your shopping habits, and take control of them by imposing a buying freeze. 90 days without buying clothes will definitely save you money, but may also make you aware that you already own plenty. Your view of fashion and marketers may change forever.

When you own fewer clothes, you can afford to buy higher quality garments, and these look better, fit better, and last longer. Choose classic styles that suit your body type, so nothing looks dated after only one season. This will enable you to avoid "fast fashion," which leads to millions of tons of textile waste each year.

With a smaller wardrobe, make sure each outfit passes the "feel good test," including casual wear. Would you feel comfortable being photographed in your outfit, or running into an old classmate? You are the curator of your wardrobe, and each piece must pass the test to be included.

For more inspiration, I highly recommend Courtney Carver's Project 333 at bemorewithless.com. Thousands of women and men have participated in this project and found that

- mornings are more peaceful with fewer choices
- it's really nice to wear your favorite clothes every day

- no one really cares that you wear the same things over and over, though they may notice that you present yourself with more self-confidence

The magic of a minimalist wardrobe happens when you shop intentionally for items you need, free from the pressures of trends and brands. The result?

You love and wear 100% of the items in your closet.

You will never find something to wear
that makes you feel beautiful, smart, or loved
until you believe you already are.
And once you believe,
you won't need it from your clothes.
When you find your confidence and worth
on the inside instead of the outside,
you'll have better things to talk about
than "what to wear."

Courtney Carver

24. X-Ray Vision Clears Hidden Clutter

We're finite creatures. We have only so much time, money, space, and energy.

But our modern consumer society offers a dizzying array of merchandise. This can have several possible effects:

- The constant influx of new products catches our attention and makes us greedy, and so we buy more than we need.

- Endless sales and clearances make everything look like a "bargain," and so we buy more than we need.

- The difficulty of making the "perfect" choice can be overwhelming, even paralyzing. We're unsure, and so we buy more than we need.

- We can't locate something essential among the clutter of past purchases, so even though we own three such items, we buy more than we need.

The load of unused items becomes a physical weight, and may cause guilt or regret. We try to hide it away in boxes, bins, drawers, closets, basements, attics, and under the bed, but it's all still there, nagging at us.

Feng Shui practitioners say that hidden clutter affects your home's energy. It makes sense that unused items create inertia. Clutter keeps you stuck in the past, or demonstrates your fears about the future.

Clutter reveals indecision and procrastination.

Items that are used *move* from one place to another. Dishes and cookware are used, become dirty, get washed, and are returned to the cupboard. Clothing is worn, dirtied, laundered, and returned to a drawer or the closet. Tools, appliances, books, photos, knickknacks, or other things that sit in one place for a long time may simply be clutter. Does your home contain shelves, drawers, closets, maybe even *entire rooms* where nothing comes or goes? That staleness and stagnation must be cleared away.

Don't let hidden clutter trap you and drag you down. Pretend you have x-ray vision to see what's hidden, and pull it out into the open. Ask yourself "Do I need this? Does it bring something positive to my life?" Be honest. Don't let yourself make excuses. Go through things at your own pace, but go through them.

Here's a decluttering clue: **you like the things you use over and over more than the things just sitting at the back of a closet.** The dusty items are not the ones you need and love.

Don't look at each item and ask if it sparks joy or memories. At one point it probably did, which is why it's cluttering your cupboard. **Enforce a use-it-or-lose-it guideline.**

Those hidden things, the ones you keep just because you've had them for so long, or because someone gave them to you, or because your fear has made you keep them "just in case," aren't doing you any good. Let them go, and they might be useful to someone else.

Having less will highlight the items you actually use and enjoy.

Just like an undertow,
clutter has an energetic drag on your life.
The good news is that you can
throw yourself a life preserver
by simplifying.

Laurel Vespi

---

25. You Are Enough

> I thought I was taking action
> when all I was really doing
> was taking out my credit card.
>
> Anthony Ongaro

One of the ways that advertisers keep us buying is by creating the feeling that we could be the people we want to be if only we had a new car, a better phone, more stylish clothing, a sexier perfume, or an exotic vacation. We are constantly encouraged to look for change and improvement outside ourselves.

We want to believe that our next purchase will solve our problems. And it's so much easier to swipe a card or click-to-ship than it is to do the hard work of changing ourselves. I know this first hand, because I keep losing the same 30 pounds over and over again.

But you can't buy change.

Change only happens when you figure out the motivations and habits that got you where you are, and create new beliefs and practices that get you where you want to go. This is the only way to achieve change. It can't be found in a store.

How many purchases have we made hoping they would make all the difference?

- Cookbooks and diet plans we thought would help us lose weight
- Gym memberships and fitness apps we thought would help us get in shape
- Clothing and hair styles we thought would make us look thinner, younger, or more successful
- Big-screen TVs and gaming systems we thought would create more family time

I'm not saying these things are bad. Some of them could be valuable tools, but only if we actually put them to use. We can't buy our way to health, thinness, or happy relationships. It's an inside job.

It's not what I own, but what I do, that really matters.

The good news is that I *can* make these changes if I choose. I don't need an exercise bike to get in shape; I have a body in decent working order that can stretch, lift, walk, and become stronger if I just use it more. I don't need special diet food or a stack of cookbooks to get thinner; I know that eating more fruits and vegetables while cutting out desserts and snacks will result in weight loss. I don't need more tools; I have the ability within myself to become the person I want to be.

Dear aspiring minimalist, you are enough! You have enough. You don't need to buy something to improve your life. You need to tap into your own desires, creativity, and determination.

What's holding you back? Is it your belief that you *aren't* enough, that you don't actually have what it takes to make a change? I've had the exact same feelings: "I've been obese for a long time; I'll always be obese." "I'm in late middle age; I'm too old to make a change." "This relationship is already distant and cold; probably nothing I do can improve it."

There are a million excuses for avoiding change, because change is hard. It means leaving our familiar comfort zone. It means risking failure.

But if we never try, we've already failed.

My father used to put it this way: "Can't never did anything." "I can't" often serves as a cover-up for "That would take too much time/effort," or "I'd embarrass myself if I tried." Saying "I can't" over and over eventually causes you to believe you are incapable, and locks you inside of a box. Too often, when I say "I can't," I really mean "I choose not to."

Let's flip my dad's saying around: "Can always does something." **Now that opens doors.**

Start by establishing a small action to complete every day – something that, over the course of a few weeks, has the potential to become a strong habit.

- Make a big green salad your go-to lunch.
- Do five minutes of stretching or yoga as soon as you wake up.
- Replace your customary venti Frappuccino with a tall latte.
- Pleasantly greet that problematic colleague every morning.
- Take a short walk at the top of every hour.
- Refuse to bring your phone to the dinner table.
- Declutter one item.

You may think that such a small action won't make much difference. But if you keep taking those little steps, you *will* eventually move closer to your goal. Keep doing what you have always done, and a year from now you'll still be in exactly the same place.

Wouldn't you rather look back and be glad you took that first, tiny step today?

Buying stuff will never make you something you are not. **But you are enough.** You *can* achieve your goals, a step at a time.

I know of no more encouraging fact
than the unquestionable ability of man
to elevate his life by conscious endeavor.

Henry David Thoreau

144

26. Zero Waste

Don't you hate walking through a park and seeing garbage on the ground?   Or garbage tossed along the highway?   Is there anything uglier?

Well, actually, yes there is.   The plastic soup that infiltrates gigantic areas of our oceans, chokes marine life, and allows toxins to enter the food chain may be a problem on par with global warming.

Plastic is wonderful for some things.   I'm thankful for polycarbonate lenses that make my eyeglasses lighter, thinner, and more durable than glass would be. Sterile plastic packaging and disposable medical items prevent food contamination, reduce the chance of infection, and save lives.   Plastic insulation and sealants make buildings more energy efficient, while plastics used in cars dramatically increase miles per gallon.

But the indiscriminate use of plastics has created serious ecological problems.

Both manufacturing and waste disposal put a strain on the environment. Even recycling uses resources and causes pollution, but alarmingly, the vast majority of plastic is never recycled. Much of it enters our waterways. It may be used for only a few hours (or a few minutes!), but it takes hundreds of years to decompose.

One way to begin to address this problem is simply to reduce waste. A zero waste lifestyle aims to create no trash. Instead of a linear economy, where we take resources from the earth and then dump them, the goal is a circular economy, where we reduce our use of disposable items, reuse as much as possible, recycle what we must, and compost the rest.

Obviously, this change isn't made overnight. It's a goal we can work toward, and minimalism can help.

A minimalist is mindful about purchases.

Minimalists already know that we don't actually *need* everything that is sold to us. We don't need multiple cleaners or beauty products. We don't need 3 staplers or 40 cheap plastic pens. We don't need 36 pairs of shoes or 8 blue sweaters. We don't need the latest electronic device if what we have is perfectly good.

A minimalist values quality over quantity.

Quality items last longer and are replaced less often. A minimalist might be more likely to reuse a vintage piece of solid wood furniture than buy a new item made of fiberboard. A well-made, classically-styled piece of clothing would suit a minimalist wardrobe more than multiple fast fashion items.

33 Additional Ways to Waste Less

1. Replace plastic shopping bags with reusable totes.
Use them at the grocery store and everywhere else you shop.

2. Replace plastic produce bags with reusable mesh bags.

3. Opt for items with minimal packaging.
Avoid snack packs and individually wrapped products. Buy pantry items from bulk bins when possible, and be sure to bring your own reusable storage containers. Support brands that avoid excessive packaging.

4. Buy food more consciously to avoid waste.
Each year, we discard millions of tons of expired food while millions of people go hungry. Avoid buying economy sizes if you're unlikely to use them, and shop every few days for immediate needs, rather than stockpiling. Serve smaller portions that will actually be consumed, and compost as many food scraps as possible.

5. Replace plastic wrap and paper lunch bags.
Use a bento box or reusable snack and sandwich bags.

6. Replace plastic straws with a stainless steel straw.
Or simply do without.

7. Avoid fast food, with its disposable cups, lids, and plastic utensils and containers.
Eat at home or in a restaurant that uses real plates, cups, and silverware.

8. Avoid Styrofoam and plastic takeout containers.
Bring some of your own storage containers to the restaurant.

9. Replace plastic utensils with the real thing, even on picnics.

10. Avoid paper plates.
It's surprisingly affordable to rent real plates, cups, and silverware for a party, rather than using disposables. Or you might be able to borrow what you need.

11. Stop using disposable cups, lids, and sleeves at your coffee shop.
Ask the barista to prepare and serve your latte in a mug. I'm always sorry to see the predominance of takeaway cups used by people who have stayed in the store.

12. Avoid making coffee with single-use pods.
Use a drip machine or a pour-over setup instead. Use a stainless steel filter instead of paper.

13. Replace tea bags with a stainless steel strainer and loose leaf tea packed in a tin.

14. Avoid bottled water.
Fill a reusable bottle from the tap.

15. Replace paper towels with cloth to wipe up spills.

16. Avoid plastic sponges.
Use washable dish cloths, and change them daily.

17. Replace paper napkins with cloth napkins.

18. Replace paper baking cups with silicone cups.

19. Stop buying throwaway razors.
Shave with an electric razor or a reusable one with replaceable blades.

20. Replace plastic toothbrushes with compostable bamboo toothbrushes.

21. Be frugal with personal care products.
Use smaller amounts of shampoo, facial cleanser, and other potions. You'll find that less is still enough for the job, and you'll save money while using fewer containers.

22. Consider using disposable diapers and wipes only when traveling.
Use cloth diapers and wipes at home. I know it's a big commitment, but earlier generations managed it even without washing machines and tumble dryers.

23. Consider using a menstrual cup or cloth pads instead of disposable feminine hygiene products.

24. Consider using facial tissues only when you're sick.
Carry a handkerchief the rest of the time.

25. Replace dryer sheets with wool dryer balls.

26. Use refilled ink cartridges in your printer.
Print only when absolutely necessary.

27. Use refillable pens and mechanical pencils.

28. Invest in rechargeable batteries.

29. Reuse paper gift wrap and bags.
You could also present your gift in a small cloth tote.

30. Choose glitter-free paper items and makeup.
Glitter is a microplastic that is dangerous to sea life.

31. Consolidate online orders and request that they be shipped in a single box.
This reduces packaging and the airline emissions generated by multiple shipments.

32. Generally choose wood and fabric toys over plastic.
Exceptions might be made when detail is important, since plastic can be more intricately fashioned than wood. Toys such as Lego are also versatile, durable, and even heirloom-worthy (my grandson plays with decades-old bricks used by his mother and uncle).

33. Replace belongings less often.

Treat and soak stains. Repair things when they break. Take care of what you own so you can use it longer.

I do not yet practice all of these suggestions, but I'm working toward that goal. Why not pick a disposable item you use regularly and replace it with a reusable version? Practice for several weeks until it becomes a habit. Then choose another item and go on from there.

Francine Jay, author of *Lightly*, suggests that one key to generating less waste is awareness. To that end, make your kitchen trash can your only trash can. You'll begin to see exactly how much you throw away. Challenge yourself to extend the time it takes to fill a trash bag to a week or more. Such a goal will inspire you to reduce your purchases while reusing, recycling, and composting as much as possible.

Coda

> Excess possessions do not
> increase happiness –
> they distract us from the things that do!
>
> Joshua Becker

As we have seen, minimalism is about living consciously and with only the things you need. Minimalists focus less on material possessions and more on relationships, experiences, and the memories created over time.

That doesn't mean you have to give up all of your belongings or your dreams of owning a house or a car. It does mean that you don't put much stock in the idea that what you own will bring you happiness.

Minimalism is freeing. It helps you slow down and look at life from a different perspective. It teaches you to focus on what is truly important to you so you can find lasting fulfillment.

When you're a minimalist, you

- consume less
- eliminate discontent
- discover your purpose
- pursue your dreams and passions
- deepen your relationships
- value your health
- live moment by moment
- contribute to the world

We all have to consume.

We all need food, shelter, clothing, education, transportation, and other essentials. But we're constantly bombarded by advertisers who want us to buy more. Buying more is what keeps our culture humming along. But buying more is also keeping us in bondage to work, chores, busyness, and debt. Buying more creates problems like comparisons, dissatisfaction, worry, waste, and evils like environmental destruction and unjust labor practices.

But joy doesn't come from things. Joy comes from the people we love, the experiences we've relished, the exercise of our talents and creativity, and all the many beauties that are worth our attention.

Join me! Make the choice to own and do less so that you can love, create, and experience **MORE**.

Instead of thinking I am losing something
when I clear clutter,
I dwell on what I might gain.

Lisa J. Shultz